MAVOR'S SPELLING-BOOK.

FRONTISPIECE.

The

English Spelling-Book

ACCOMPANIED BY

A PROGRESSIVE SERIES

OF

EASY AND FAMILIAR LESSONS

BY

WILLIAM MAVOR, LL.D.

ILLUSTRATED BY KATE GREENAWAY

WORTH PRESS

CAMBRIDGE

This edition first published in 2013 by Worth Press
Ltd, Cambridge, England.
www.worthpress.co.uk

Previously published by George Routledge & Sons
in 1885.

Introduction by Gill Davies, Cover and
Endpaper design all © Worth Press Ltd, 2013.

British Library Cataloguing in Publication Data
A catalogue record for this book is available from
the British Library.

ISBN: 978-1-84931-076-5
10 9 8 7 6 5 4 3 2 1

Publisher's Note Every effort has been made to
ensure the accuracy of the information presented
in this book. The publisher will not assume liability
for damages caused by inaccuracies in the data and
makes no warranty whatsoever expressed or implied.
The publisher welcomes comments and corrections
from readers, emailed to info@worthpress.co.uk,
which will be considered for incorporation in
future editions. Every effort has been made to
trace copyright holders and seek permission to use
illustrative and other material. The publisher wishes
to apologize for any inadvertent errors or omissions
and would be glad to rectify these in future editions.

The images used in this book come from either the
public domain or from the public commons unless
otherwise stated.

Printed and bound by Imago Publishing in China.

INTRODUCTION

he *English Spelling Book* by William Fordyce Mavor was originally published in 1801 – to be followed by numerous editions. This is a facsimile reproduction of an enchanting version originally published in 1885, with glorious illustrations by Kate Greenaway. The pair never actually collaborated as Kate was not even born until some nine years after William's demise but her illustrations gave the book a new life force, reaching a far wider audience than its predecessors. It represents a high point in the creation of illustrated ABCs for children that had developed along with the spread of education for all classes, not just the wealthier ones.

English language and spelling mutated through a maelstrom of politics, economics, laziness, greediness and accident. Few other languages proffer as many spelling inconsistencies and irregularities – even a cursory exploration reveals a rich and complex history. Many words have ancient origins but both spellings and pronunciation evolved from the Dark Ages onwards. After 1066 and the Norman invasion, French became the official language of England and for some three centuries only a few monks continued to write in English. However, uneducated labourers still conversed in their home tongue, thus keeping the language alive.

England reasserted its own identity during the

latter 1300s but its Anglo-Saxon language base continued its evolution in the hands of writers such as Geoffrey Chaucer – and William Tyndale who translated the Bible into modern English in 1525. These worthy authors tried to retain consistent spelling but French and Latin tendencies still permeated. Meanwhile the early London printers were often from foreign climes and misspelled many words. Often paid by the line, they would insert additional letters into words to extend the text and so earn more money. Many of these errors eventually became accepted English spelling.

Spelling had become increasingly unrelated to pronunciation, largely because printing clung to the late Middle English forms just when various changes were dramatically altering pronunciation. In particular, the 'Great Vowel Shift' meant that the three long vowels (i, e and a) assumed values similar to their Latin or continental counterparts but this did not penetrate English spelling 'standards'.

Bibles were often used as teaching aids but different editions proffered a variety of spellings, thus adding to the chaos – as did the importation of many Latin and Greek words. Samuel Johnson's dictionary of 1755 rigidly fixed spellings – now based on his tome rather than phonics or logic.

One of the earliest alphabet teaching aids was the hornbook, made from parchment stretched over a paddle and covered with a fine layer of cow's horn to protect it. It included both upper and lower case and very often the Lord's Prayer as a familiar text for purposes of comparison. One novel learning aid was a set of gingerbread letters to serve as both reward and motivation.

Through the 1700s and 1800s, battledores became very popular: the alphabet was printed on thin folded cardboard with capital and lower case letters mixed up to better test a child's knowledge. A short story, word lists and a prayer might be included. Illustrations depicted both scenes and familiar single objects.

Primers, readers and spellers followed: several printed paper pages displayed the alphabet, syllable lists, common words, Biblical texts and stories with a moral message. In due course, numbers, animals and household objects appeared. There might also be notes on pronunciation, grammar and arithmetic, as well as advice to young persons and lists of English royalty.

During the later 1800s, ABC books became more widely written and published, as books for young children grew ever more popular and available. These included stories and illustrations to add to the fun. Early learning was suddenly more than just a tedious drill. In 1871 Edward Lear had an alphabet published together with his Nonsense verse while Kate Greenaway's works introduced gentle humour and affection into the educational process.

The Author: William Fordyce Mavor (1758–1837) was a renowned compiler of educational works. Born at New Deer, Aberdeenshire, he became an assistant in a school at Burford, Oxfordshire, at the age of 17 and later taught at Woodstock, helping the Duke of Marlborough's children develop their reading and writing skills. He took holy orders in 1781 and eight years later the duke granted him the vicarage of Hurley, Berkshire, which he retained until his death. With his LL.D degree conferred upon him by the university of Aberdeen, he later served at the rectory of Stonesfield and at Bladon-with-Woodstock. He was licensed by the bishop to the head-mastership of Woodstock grammar school and in 1808 was elected mayor of Woodstock; he served this office ten times. He died in 1837 and there is a tablet to his memory by his Woodstock grave. Mavor was a successful compiler of educational books, many of which saw numerous editions and *The English Spelling Book* – originally published in 1801 – was especially popular. He also invented a system of shorthand.

The Artist: Kate Greenaway (1846–1901)

Illustrator and writer Kate Greenaway studied at what is now London's Royal College of Art. Her first book of verses, *Under the Window*, was published in 1879 – and soon became a bestseller. Her paintings often depicted young boys not yet in trousers (according to the conventions of the time) and girls in smock-frocks, pinafores and straw bonnets. Her work inspired Liberty of London to have actual children's clothes made that reflected her images. Encouraged by John Ruskin's enthusiasm for her art and the unprecedented success of her books, Kate Greenaway created many works and became a veritable 1800s icon, with her distinct style instantly recognizable. She researched both costumes and backgrounds in great detail and was elected to membership of the Royal Institute of Painters in Water Colours – but died of cancer when aged only 55. The Kate Greenaway Medal, established in her honour in 1955, is awarded annually in the UK to a worthy children's illustrator while her beautiful picture books have held their popularity through to today.

A a   B b

C c   D d

E e   F f

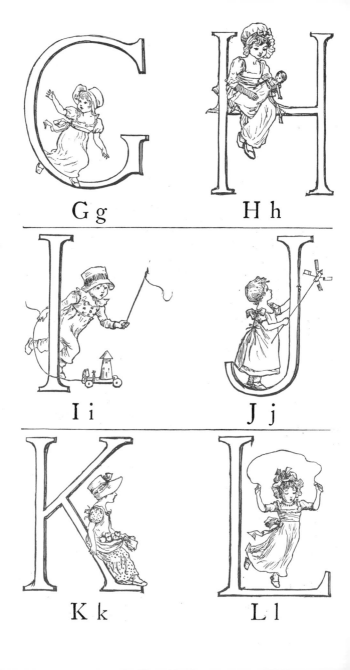

G g

H h

I i

J j

K k

L l

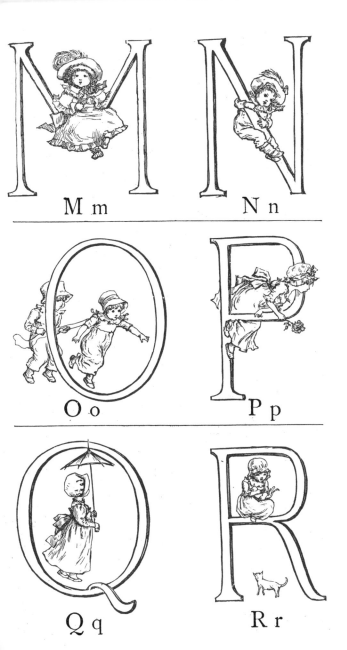

M m

N n

O o

P p

Q q

R r

S s

T t

U u

V v

W w

X x

Y y   Z z

The Italic Letters.

A B C D E F G H I J K L M N O P Q R S T U V W X Y Z

a b c d e f g h i j k l m n o p q r s t u v w x y z

The Vowels are, *a e i o u y*

The Consonants are, *b c d f g h j k l m n p q r s t v w x z*

Diphthongs, &c.

Æ	Œ	æ	œ	&	&c.
AE	OE	ae	oe	and	*et cætera.*

Old English Capitals.

𝔄 𝔅 ℭ 𝔇 𝔈 𝔉 𝔊 ℌ 𝔍 𝔎 𝔏 𝔐 𝔑 𝔒 𝔓 𝔔 𝔕 𝔖 𝔗 𝔘 𝔙 𝔚 𝔛 𝔜 ℨ

Old English, small.

a b c d e f g h i j k l m n o p q r s t u v w x y z

Arabic Numerals.

1 2 3 4 5 6 7 8 9 0

Roman Numerals.

I. II. III. IV. V. VI. VII. VIII. IX. X. XI. XII. XIII. XIV. XV. XVI. XIX. XX. C. D. M.

Lesson 1.

ba	be	bi	bo	bu	by
ca	ce	ci	co	cu	cy
da	de	di	do	du	dy
fa	fe	fi	fo	fu	fy

Lesson 2.

ga	ge	gi	go	gu	gy
ha	he	hi	ho	hu	hy
ja	je	ji	jo	ju	jy
ka	ke	ki	ko	ku	ky
la	le	li	lo	lu	ly

Lesson 3.

ma	me	mi	mo	rnu	my
na	ne	ni	no	nu	ny
pa	pe	pi	po	pu	py
ra	re	ri	ro	ru	ry
sa	se	si	so	su	sy

Lesson 4.

ta	te	ti	to	tu	ty
va	ve	vi	vo	vu	vy
wa	we	wi	wo	wu	wy
ya	ye	yi	yo	yu	yy
za	ze	zi	zo	zu	zy

Lesson 5.

ab	ac	ad	af	ag	al
eb	ec	ed	ef	eg	el
ib	ic	id	if	ig	il
ob	oc	od	of	og	ol
ub	uc	ud	uf	ug	ul

Lesson 6.

am	an	ap	ar	as	at
em	en	ep	er	es	et
im	in	ip	ir	is	it
om	on	op	or	os	ot
um	un	up	ur	us	ut

Lesson 7.

ax	am	on	yo	me	so
ex	of	no	he	be	wo
ix	ye	my	at	to	lo
ox	by	as	up	ye	go
ux	an	or	ho	we	do

Lesson 8.

in	so	am	an	if	ha
ay	oy	my	ye	be	as
oh	it	on	go	no	us
me	we	up	to	us	lo

Lesson 9.

He is up.	We go in.	So do we.
It is so.	Lo we go.	As we go.
Do ye so.	I go up.	If it be so,

Lesson 10.

I am he.	So do I.	I do go.
He is in.	It is an ox.	Is he on.
I go on.	He or me.	We do so.

Lesson 11.

Ah me!	Be it so.	Do so.
I am off.	I am to go.	It is I.
Ye do go.	So it is.	He is to go.

Lesson 12.

Ye go by us.	Ah me, it is so.
It is my ox.	If ye do go in.
Do as we do.	So do we go on.

Lesson 13.

If he is to go.	Is it so or no?
I am to do so.	If I do go in.
It is to be on.	Am I to go on?

Lesson 1.

bad	lad	pad	bed	led	red
dad	mad	sad	fed	ned	wed

Lesson 2.

bid	hid	lid	god	nod	bud
did	kid	rid	hod	rod	mud

Lesson 3.

big	wig	dog	jog	hug	pug
dig	bog	fog	bug	jug	rug
fig	log	hog	dug	mug	tug

Lesson 4.

can	pan	zan	hen	din	kin
fan	ran	den	men	fin	pin
man	van	fen	pen	gin	sin

Lesson 5.

cap	lap	pap	tap	lip	rip
gap	map	rap	dip	nip	sip
hap	nap	sap	hip	pip	tip

Lesson 6.

tar	far	mar	car	fir	cur
bar	jar	par	war	sir	pur

Lesson 7.

bat	mat	bet	let	wet	kit
cat	pat	fet	met	bit	sit
fat	rat	get	net	fit	dot
hat	sat	jet	pet	hit	wit

Lesson 8.

got	jot	not	rot	but	nut
hot	lot	pot	sot	hut	put

Lesson 9.

shy	fly	sly	cry	fry	try
thy	ply	bry	dry	pry	wry

Lesson 10.

for	was	dog	the	you	and
may	art	egg	see	eat	fox
are	ink	had	off	boy	has

Lessons, in Words not exceeding THREE *Letters.*

Lesson 1.	Lesson 2.
His pen is bad.	Let me get a nap.
I met a man.	My hat was on.
He has a net.	His hat is off.
We had an egg.	We are all up.

Lesson 3.

Let the cat be put in a bag.

I can eat an egg.

The dog bit my toe.

The cat and dog are at war.

Lesson 4.

You are a bad boy, if you pull off the leg of a fly.

A fox got the old hen, and ate her.

Our dog got the pig.

Do as you are bid, or it may be bad for you.

By attending to the *Leading* Sound of the Vowel, the following classification will be found to combine the advantages, both of a SPELLING and a PRONOUNCING VOCABULARY.

cart	harm	fell	bolt	bank
dart	cash	sell	colt	rank
hart	hash	tell	camp	sank
part	mash	well	damp	link
tart	rash	bill	lamp	pink
band	sash	fill	hemp	sink
hand	cast	kill	limp	wink
land	fast	mill	bump	sunk
sand	last	pill	dump	monk
hall	past	will	jump	pant
pall	bath	doll	pump	rant
tall	lath	loll	bend	lent
wall	path	dull	mend	rent
fang	balk	gull	rend	sent
gang	talk	hull	send	tent
hang	walk	bull	bind	went
rang	halt	full	find	dint
bard	malt	pull	kind	hint
card	salt	poll	mind	lint
hard	calf	roll	wind	mint
lard	half	toll	bond	herb
yard	balm	pelf	pond	verb
bark	calm	helm	fond	curb
dark	palm	help	ring	herd
hark	milk	yelp	sing	bird
lark	silk	belt	wing	third
mark	bulk	melt	long	cord
park	hulk	gilt	song	lord
barm	bell	hilt	hung	cork
farm	cell	tilt	sung	fork

ford	rasp	nigh	march	chill
fort	lisp	sigh	latch	drill
port		high	catch	skill
pork	mass		fetch	spill
	pass	warm	ditch	still
word	less	wasp	pitch	droll
work	mess	dwarf	witch	stroll
worm	hiss	wharf		
	kiss	storm	gnat	psalm
barn	miss	form	knack	whelm
yarn	moss	sort	knock	
fern	loss	quart	kneel	spelt
born		wolf	knob	spilt
corn	best	tomb	know	stilt
horn	jest	jamb		
lorn	lest	lamb	fight	thumb
morn	nest		knight	dumb
burn	rest	straw	light	
turn	vest	gnaw	might	cramp
torn	west	awl	night	stamp
worn	zest	bawl	right	clamp
	fist	owl	sight	plump
bars	mist	fowl	tight	trump
cars	host	growl	blight	
tars	most		flight	brand
	post	smith	bright	grand
dish		pith		stand
fish	dust	both	breeze	strand
wish	gust	sloth	sneeze	blend
with	must		freeze	spend
gush	rust	broth		blind
rush	cost	cloth	small	grind
	lost	froth	stall	
task	cow	moth	dwell	bring
dusk	bow		knell	cling
husk	vow	welsh	smell	fling
musk	now	haunch	spell	sting
rusk		launch	swell	swing
tusk		arch		thing
				wring

spring	thyme	scorn	brisk	man
string	scene	thorn	whisk	boy
wrong	scythe	shorn	whisp	girl
strong	scheme	sworn	clasp	egg
throng	school	sport	grasp	hen
strung	grant	smart	brass	cock
flung	slant	chart	glass	book
stung	scent	start	bless	bee
swung	spent	shirt	dress	coach
drank	flint	skirt	stress	cart
frank	blunt	spirt	bliss	pie
thank	grunt	short	dross	tart
blank	front	snort	gloss	milk
flank	board	clash	blest	tom
plank	hoard	crash	chest	sam
plant	sword	smash	crest	will
brink	shark	trash	twist	fire
clink	spark	wash	thrust	smoke
drink	snarl	quash	crust	sun
slink	twirl	brush	trust	moon
think	whirl	crush	crost	stars
drunk	churn	flush	frost	rod
trunk	stern	plush	dog	stick
rhyme				

Common Words to be known at Sight.

and	this	all	our	your	art	will
an	that	as	they	what	is	would
the	but	he	them	these	are	shall
of	no	she	their	those	was	should
for	not	it	who	there	were	may
from	with	him	whom	some	been	might
to	up	her	whole	when	have	can
on	or	we	which	be	has	could
by	if	us	you	am	had	must

Words to be known at Sight with Capitals.

The	Up	She	Might	From	Who	Your
An	Or	It	Would	That	Their	What
Of	But	Him	Shall	Whole	Them	These
And	If	Her	May	Has	Those	There
For	No	We	Can	Am	With	Was
On	All	Us	Should	Art	They	Were
To	Not	Our	Could	Is	When	Been
This	He	You	Will	Whom	Some	Have
By	As	Be	Had	Are	Which	Must

Lessons on the E *final.*

bab	babe	fir	fire	mut	mute	sid	side
ban	bane	for	fore	nam	name	sir	sire
bar	bare	gal	gale	nod	node	sit	site
bid	bide	gam	game	nor	nore	sol	sole
bil	bile	gat	gate	not	note	sur	sure
bit	bite	gor	gore	od	ode	tal	tale
can	cane	har	hare	pan	pane	tam	tame
car	care	hat	hate	par	pare	tap	tape
cap	cape	her	here	pil	pile	tar	tare
con	cone	hid	hide	pin	pine	tid	tide
cop	cope	hop	hope	pol	pole	tim	time
dal	dale	hol	hole	por	pore	ton	tone
dam	dame	kit	kite	rat	rate	top	tope
dar	dare	lad	lade	rid	ride	tub	tube
dat	date	mad	made	rip	ripe	tun	tune
din	dine	man	mane	rob	robe	van	vane
dol	dole	mar	mare	rod	rode	val	vale
dom	dome	mat	mate	rop	rope	vil	vile
dot	dote	mil	mile	rot	rote	vin	vine
fam	fame	mod	mode	rud	rude	vot	vote
fan	fane	mol	mole	rul	rule	wid	wide
fat	fate	mop	mope	sal	sale	win	wine
fin	fine	mor	more	sam	same	wir	wire

Lessons, consisting of easy words of ONE *Syllable.*

Lesson 1.

A mad ox	A wild colt	A live calf
An old man	A tame cat	A gold ring
A new fan	A lean cow	A warm muff

Lesson 2.

A fat duck	A lame pig	A good dog
He can call	You will fall	He may beg
You can tell	He must sell	I will run
I am tall	I shall dig	Tom was hot

Lesson 3.

She is well	He did laugh	He is cold
You can walk	Ride your nag	Fly your kite
Do not slip	Ring the bell	Give it me
Fill that box	Spin the top	Take you bat

Lesson 4.

Take this book	Toss that ball	Buy it for us
A good boy	A sad dog	A new whip
A bad man	A soft bed	Get your book
A dear girl	A nice cake	Go to the door
A fine lad	A long stick	Come to the fire

Lesson 5.

Speak out	Do you love me	Come and read
Do not cry	Be a good girl	Hear what I say
I love you	I like good boys	Do as you are bid
Look at it	All will love you	Mind your book

Lessons in Words of ONE *Syllable.*

Lesson 1.

Miss Jane Bond had a new doll; and her good Aunt, who bought it, gave her some cloth to make a shift for it. She gave her a coat too, and a pair of stays, and a yard of twist with a tag to it, for a lace; a pair of red shoes, and a piece of blue silk to make doll a slip, some gauze for a frock, and a broad white sash.

Now these were fine things you know; but Miss Jane had no thread, so she could not make doll's clothes when she had cut them out; but her kind Aunt gave her some thread too, and then she went hard to work, and made doll quite smart in a short time.

Lesson 2.

Please to give me a plum.   Here is one.

I want more, I want ten, if you please.
Here are ten.   Count them.   I will.   One (1),
two (2), three (3), four (4), five (5), six (6),
seven (7), eight (8), nine (9), ten (10).

Lesson 3.

I knew a nice girl, but she was not good:
she was cross, and told fibs. One day she went
out to take a walk in the fields, and tore her
frock in a bush; and when she came home, she
said she had not done it, but that the dog had
done it with his paw. Was that good?—No.

Her Aunt gave her a cake; and she thought
if John saw it, he would want to have a bit;
and she did not choose he should; so she put
it in a box and hid it, that he might not see it.
The next day she went to eat some of her cake,
but it was gone; there was a hole in the box,
and a mouse had crept in, and eat it all. She

then did cry so much that the nurse thought she was hurt; but when she told her what the mouse had done, she said she was glad of it; and that it was a bad thing to wish to eat it all, and not to give a bit to John.

Lesson 4.

Miss Rose was a good child, she did at all times what she was bid. She got all her tasks by heart, and did her work quite well. One day she had learnt a long task in her book, and done some nice work; so her Aunt said, you

are a good girl, my dear, and I will take you with me to see Miss Cox.

So Miss Rose went with her Aunt, and Miss Cox was quite glad to see her, and took her to her play-room, where they saw a Doll's house. with rooms in it; there were eight rooms; and there were in these rooms chairs, and stools, and beds, and plates, and cups, and spoons, and knives, and forks, and mugs, and a screen, and I do not know what. So Miss Rose was glad she had done her work, and said her task so well; for if she had not she would have staid at home, and lost the sight of the Doll's house.

Lesson 5.

Come, James, make haste. Now read your book. Here is a pin to point with. Do not tear the book. Spell that word. That is a good boy. Now go and play till I call you in.

Lesson 6.

The sun shines. Open your eyes, good girl.
Get up. Maid, come and dress Jane. Boil
some milk for a poor girl. Do not spill the
milk. Hold the spoon in your right hand. Do
not throw the bread on the ground. Bread is
made to eat, and you must not waste it.

Lesson 7.

Charles went out to walk in the fields; he
saw a bird, and ran to catch it; and when they
said, Do not take the poor bird; what will you
do with it? He said, I will put it in a cage and
keep it. But they told him he must not; for
they were sure he would not like to be shut up
in a cage, and run no more in the fields—why
then should the poor bird like it? So Charles
let the poor thing fly.

Lesson 8.

Here is a fine sleet cat. She purrs, and frisks, and wags her tail. Do not tease her, or she will scratch you, and make you bleed.

See what a sweet bird this is. Look at his bright eyes, his fine wings, and nice long tail.

Lesson 9.

Try to learn fast. Thank those who teach you. Strive to speak plain. Speak as if the words were your own. Do not bawl; nor yet speak in too low a voice. Speak so that all in the room may hear you. Read as you talk.

Look! there is our dog Tray. He takes good care of the house. He will bark, but he will not bite, if you do not hurt him.

Lesson 10.

Jack Hall was a good boy. He went to school, and took pains to learn as he ought. When he was in school, he kept to his books, till all his tasks were done; and then when he came out, he could play with a good heart, for he knew that he had time; and he was so kind, that all the boys were glad to play with him.

When he was one of the least boys in the school, he made all the great boys his friends; and when he grew a great boy, he was a friend to all that were less than he was. He was not once known to fight, or to use one of the boys ill, as long as he staid at school.

Be like Jack Hall, and you too will gain the love of all who know you.

Lesson 11.

A cat has soft fur and a long tail. She looks meek, but she is sly; and if she finds a rat or a mouse, she will fly at him, and kill him soon. She will catch birds and kill them.

Lesson 12.

I once saw a young girl tie a string to a bird's leg, and pull it through the yard. But it could not go so fast as she did; she ran, and it went hop, hop, to try to keep up with her, but it broke its poor leg, and there it lay on the

hard stones, and its head was hurt; and the poor bird was soon dead. So I told her maid not to let her have birds if she was to use them so ill; and she has not had one since that time.

Lesson 13.

You must not hurt live things. You should not kill poor flies, nor pull off their legs nor wings. You must not hurt bees, for they do good, and will not sting you, if you do not touch them.   All things that have life can feel as well as you can, and should not be hurt.

Lesson 14.

Tom fell in the pond; they got him out, but he was wet and cold; and his eyes were shut;

and then he was sick, and they put him to bed;
and he was long ill and weak, and could not
stand. Why did he go near the pond? He
had been told not to go, for fear he should fall
in; but he would go, and he did fall in; it was
his own fault, and he was a bad boy. Mind
and do not do the same.

Lesson 15.

Miss May makes all her friends laugh at her;
if a poor mouse runs by her, she screams for
an hour; and a bee on her frock will put her in
a fit; if a small fly should get on her hair, and
buz in her ear, she would call all in the house
to help her, as if she was hurt.

Lesson 16.

Frank Pitt was a great boy; he had such a pair of fat cheeks that he could scarce see out of his eyes, for you must know that Frank would sit and eat all day long. First he would have a great mess of rice milk, in an hour's time he would ask for bread and cheese, then he would eat loads of fruit and cakes: and as for meat and pies, if you had seen him eat them, it would have made you stare. Then he would drink as much as he eat. But Frank could not long go on so, no one can feed in this way but it must make him ill; and this was the case with Frank Pitt; nay, he was like to die; but he did get well at last, though it was a long while first.

Lesson 17.

Look at Jane, her hand is bound up in a cloth; you do not know what ails it, but I will tell you. She had a mind to try if she could poke the fire, though she had been told she must not do it; and it would have been well for her if she had not tried; for she had not strength for such work as that, and she fell with her hand on the bar of the grate; which burnt her much, and gave her great pain; and she cannot work, or play, or do the least thing with her hand. It was a sad thing not to mind what was said to her.

Lesson 18.

What are eyes for ?—To see with.

What are ears for ?—To hear with.

What is a tongue for ?—To talk with.

What are teeth for ?—To eat with.

What is a nose for ?—To smell with.

What are legs for ?—To walk with.

What are books for ?—To learn with.

Exercises in Words of ONE SYLLABLE *containing the* DIPHTHONGS.

ai, ei, oi, ea, oa, ie, ue, ui, au, ou.

aid	air	spoil	speak	leap
laid	fair	coin	screak	reap
maid	hair	join	squeak	cheap
paid	pair	loin	deal	ear
waid	chair	groin	meal	dear
braid	stair	joint	peal	fear
staid	bait	point	seal	hear
gain	gait	pea	teal	near
main	wait		steal	sear
pain	said		sweal	year
rain	saith	sea	beam	blear
blain		tea	ream	clear
chain	neigh	flea	seam	smear
brain	weigh	plea	team	spear
drain	eight	each	bream	ease
grain	weight	beach	cream	pease
train	reign	leach	dream	tease
slain	vein	peach	fleam	please
stain	feign	reach	gleam	seas
swain	rein	teach	steam	fleas
twain	heir	bleach	scream	cease
sprain	their	breach	stream	peace
strain	height	preach	beam	grease
faint		beak	dean	east
paint	voice	peak	mean	beast
saint	choice	leak	lean	feast
plaint	void	weak	clean	least
plait	soil	bleak	glean	eat
faith	toil	freak	heap	beat
	broil	sneak		

feat	hearth	soar	lies	plough
heat	heart	boast	pies	bough
meat	great	roast	ties	bound
neat	bear	toast	quest	found
peat	pear	boat	guest	hound
seat	coach	coat	suit	pound
teat	poach	goat	fruit	round
bleat	roach	moat	juice	sound
cheat	goad	float	sluice	wound
treat	load	throat	bruise	ground
wheat	road	broad	cruise	
realm	toad	groat	build	sour
dealt	woad	brief	guild	flour
health	loaf	chief	built	bout
wealth	oak	grief	guilt	gout
stealth	coal	thief	guise	doubt
breast	foal	liege	fraud	lout
sweat	goal	mien	daunt	pout
threat	shoal	siege	jaunt	rout
death	roam	field	haunt	bought
breath	foam	wield	vaunt	thought
search	loam	yield	caught	ought
earl	loan	shield	taught	though
pearl	moan	fierce	fraught	four
earn	groan	pierce	aunt	pour
learn	oar	tierce		tough
earth	boar	grieve	loud	rough
dearth	roar	thieve	cloud	your

Words of Arbitrary Sounds.

ache	laugh	lieu	drachm	quoif
adze	toe	quay	hymn	aye
aisle	choir	schism	nymph	quoit
yacht	pique	czar	gaol	ewe

Words Accented on the FIRST *Syllable.*

OBSERVATION.   The double (″) when it unavoidably occurs, shows tha the following consonant is to be pronounced in both syllables; as co″-py, pronounced cop-py.

Ab-bot	am-ple	aw-ful	base-ness
ab-ject	an-chor	a-zure	ba-sin
a-ble	an-gel	Bab-bler	bask-et
ab-sent	an-ger	ba-by	bat-ten
obs-tract	an-gle	back-bite	bat-tle
ac-cent	an-gry	back-ward	bawl-ing
a″-cid	an-cle	ba-con	bea-con
a-corn	an-swer	bad-ger	bea-dle
ac-rid	an-vil	bad-ness	beard-less
act-ive	a-ny	baf-fle	bear-er
act-or	ap-ple	bag-gage	beast-ly
act-ress	a-pril	bai-liff	beat-er
ad-age	a-pron	ba-ker	beau-ty
ad-der	apt-ness	ba-lance	bed-ding
ad-dle	ar-bour	bald-ness	bee-hive
ad-vent	arch-er	bal-lad	beg-gar
ad-verb	arc-tic	bal-last	be-ing
ad-verse	ar-dent	band-age	bed-lam
af-ter	ar-dour	band-box	bed-time
a-ged	ar-gent	ban-ish	bel-fry
a-gent	ar-gue	bank-er	bel-man
a″-gile	ar-id	bank-rupt	bel-low
a-gue	ar-mour	ban-ner	ber-ry
ail-ment	ar-my	ban-quet	be-som
ai-ry	ar-row	ban-ter	bet-ter
al-ley	art-ful	bap-tism	bi-as
al-mond	art-ist	bar-ber	bi-ble
al-o″e	art-less	bare-foot	big-ness
al-so	ash-es	bar-gain	bi″-got
al-tar	as-pect	bark-ing	bind-er
al-ter	as-pen	bar-ley	bind-ing
al-um	as-sets	bar-on	bird-lime
al-ways	asth-ma	bar-ren	birth-day
am-ber	au-dit	bar-row	bish-op
am-bush	au-thor	bar-ter	bit-ter

bit-tern	brace-let	bum-per	ceil-ing
black-en	brack-et	bun-dle	cel-lar
black-ness	brack-ish	bun-gle	cen-sure
blame-less	bram-ble	bur-den	cen-tre
blank-et	bran-dish	bur-gess	cer-tain
bleak-ness	brave-ly	burn-er	chal-lenge
bleat-ing	brawl-ing	bush-el	cham-ber
bleed-ing	bra-zen	bus-tle	chan-cel
blem-ish	break-fast	butch-er	chand-ler
bless-ing	breast-plate	but-ler	chang-er
blind-ness	breath-less	but-ter	chan-nel
blis-ter	breed-ing	bux-om	chap-el
blood-shed	brew-er	Cab-bage	chap-lain
blos-som	bri-ber	cab-in	chap-ter
blow-ing	brick-bat	ca-ble	char-coal
blue-ness	brick-kiln	cad-dy	char-ger
blun-der	bri-dal	call-ing	charm-er
blus-ter	bride-maid	cam-bric	charm-ing
board-er	bri-dle	can-cel	char-ter
boast-er	brief-ly	can-cer	chas-ten
bob-bin	bri-ar	can-did	chat-tels
bod-kin	bright-ness	can-dle	chat-ter
bo"-dy	brim-stone	can-non	cheap-ness
boil-er	bring-er	can-vas	cheat-er
bold-ness	bris-tle	ca-per	cheer-ful
bol-ster	brit-tle	cap-tain	chem-ist
bond-age	bro-ken	cap-tive	cher-ish
bon-fire	bro-ker	car-case	cher-ry
bon-net	bru-tal	care-ful	chest-nut
bo-ny	bru-tish	care-less	chief-ly
boo-by	bub-ble	car-rot	child-hood
book-ish	buck-et	car-pet	child-ish
boor-ish	buc-kle	cart-er	chil-dren
boo-ty	bud-get	carv-er	chim-ney
bor-der	buf-fet	case-ment	chis-el
bor-row	bug-bear	cas-ket	chop-ping
bot-tle	bu-gle	cas-tle	chuc-kle
bot-tom	bul-let	cause-way	churl-ish
bound-less	bul-rush	caus-tic	churn-ing
boy-ish	bul-wark	ce-dar	ci-der

cin-der	com-ment	crea-ture	dead-ly
ci-pher	com-merce	cred-it	death-less
cir-cle	com-mon	crib-bage	debt-or
cis-tern	com-pact	crook-ed	de-cent
ci″-ty	com-pass	cross-ness	del-uge
clam-ber	com-pound	cru-el	di-et
clam-my	com-rade	crum-ple	dif-fer
clam-our	con-cave	crus-ty	dim-ness
clap-per	con-cert	crys-tal	dim-ple
clar-et	con-cord	cud-gel	din-ner
clas-sic	con-course	cul-prit	dis-cord
clat-ter	con-flict	cun-ning	dis-mal
clean-ly	con-gress	cup-board	dis-tance
clear-ness	con-quer	cu-rate	do-er
cler-gy	con-quest	cur-dle	do-nor
clev-er	con-stant	curl-ing	doubt-ful
cli-ent	con-sul	cur-rant	doubt-less
cli-mate	con-test	cur-rent	dow-ny
clo-ser	con-tract	cur-tain	drag-gle
clo-set	con-vent	curv-ed	dra-gon
clou-dy	con-vert	cus-tard	dra-per
clo-ver	con-vex	cus-tom	draw-er
clown-ish	con-vict	cut-ler	dread-ful
clus-ter	cool-ness	cy-press	dream-er
clum-sy	coop-er	Dab-ble	drop-sy
cob-bler	cop-per	dan-ger	drum-mer
cob-nut	co″-py	dag-ger	drunk-ard
cob-web	cor-ner	dai-ly	duke-dom
cock-pit	cost-ly	dain-ty	dul-ness
cof-fee	cot-ton	dai-ry	du-ty
cold-ness	cov-er	dam-age	dwel-ling
col-lar	coun-cil	dam-ask	dwin-dle
col-lege	coun-sel	dam-sel	Ea-ger
col-our	coun-ter	dan-cer	ea-gle
com-bat	coun-ty	dan-gle	east-er
come-ly	court-ly	dark-ness	eat-er
com-er	cow-ard	das-tard	ear-ly
com-et	cou-sin	daz-zle	earth-en
com-fort	crack-er	dear-ly	ech-o
com-ma	craf-ty	dear-ness	ef-fort

ei-ther
el-bow
el-der
em-blem
em-pire
emp-ty
end-less
en-ter
en-voy
en-vy
e-qual
er-ror
es-say
es-sence
e-ven
ev-er
e-vil
ex-it
eye-sight
eye-sore
Fa-ble
fa-bric
fac-ing
fac-tor
fag-got
faint-ness
faith-ful
false-hood
fam-ine
fam-ish
fa-mous
fan-cy
farm-er
fas-ten
fa-tal
fath-er
fa-vour
fear-ful
feath-er
fee-ble

feel-ing
fel-low
fel-on
fe-male
fen-cer
fen-der
fer-tile
fet-ter
fe-ver
fid-dle
fig-ure
fi-nal
fin-ger
fin-ish
firm-ness
fix-ed
flab-by
fla-grant
flan-nel
fla-vour
flo-rist
flow-er
flut-ter
fol-low
fol-ly
fool-ish
foot-step
fore-cast
fore-most
fore-sight
fore-head
for-est
for-mer
fort-night
for-tune
found-er
foun-tain
fow-ler
fra-grant
free-ly

fren-zy
friend-ly
frig-ate
fros-ty
fruit-ful
full-er
fun-nel
fun-ny
fur-nace
fur-nish
fur-row
fur-ther
fu-ry
fu-tile
fu-ture
Gain-ful
gal-lant
gal-lon
gal-lop
gam-ble
game-ster
gam-mon
gan-der
gar-den
gar-ment
gar-ner
gar-nish
gar-ret
gar-ter
gath-er
gau-dy
ga-zer
gen-der
gen-tile
gen-tle
gen-try
ges-ture
get-ting
gi-ant
gib-bet

gid-dy
gig-gle
gild-er
gild-ing
gim-let
gin-ger
gir-dle
girl-ish
giv-er
glad-ness
glean-er
glim-mer
gloo-my
glo-ry
glos-sy
glut-ton
gob-let
god-ly
go-er
gold-en
gos-pel
gos-sip
gou-ty
grace-ful
gram-mar
gras-sy
gra-tis
gra-ver
gra-vy
grea-sy
great-ly
great-ness
gree-dy
green-ish
greet-ing
griev-ance
griev-ous
grind-er
gris-ly
groan-ing

gro-cer
ground-less
gruff-ness
guilt-less
guil-ty
gun-ner
gus-ty
gut-ter
Hab-it
hack-ney
had-dock
hail-stone
hai-ry
halt-er
ham-let
ham-per
hand-ful
hand-maid
hand-some
han-dy
hang-in
hap-pen
hap-py
har-ass
har-bour
hard-en
har-dy
harm-ful
harm-less
har-ness
har-row
har-vest
has-ten
hat-ter
hate-ful
haugh-ty
haz-ard
ha-zel
ha-zy
hea″-dy

heal-ing
hear-ing
heart-less
hea-then
heav-en
hea″-vy
heed-ful
hel-met
help-er
help-ful
help-less
herb-age
herds-man
her-mit
her-ring
hic-cup
hil-ly
hin-der
hire-ling
hob-ble
hogs-head
hold-fast
hol-land
hol-low
ho-ly
hom-age
home-ly
hon-est
hon-our
hope-ful
hope-less
hor-rid
hor-ror
host-ess
hos-tile
hot-house
hour-ly
house-hold
hu-man
hum-ble

hu-mour
hun-ger
hunt-er
hur-ry
hurt-ful
I-dler
i-dol
im-age
in-cense
in-come
in-dex
in-fant
ink-stand
in-mate
in-quest
in-road
in-sect
in-sult
in-sight
in-stance
in-stant
in-to
in-voice
i-ron
is-sue
i-tem
Jag-ged
jeal-ous
jel-ly
jest-er
Je-sus
jew-el
jew-ish
jin-gle
join-er
jol-ly
jour-nal
jour-ney
joy-ful
joy-less

judg-ment
jug-gle
jui-cy
ju-ry
just-ice
Keep-er
ken-nel
ker-nel
ket-tle
key-hole
kin-dle
kind-ness
king-dom
kit-chen
kna-vish
kneel-ing
know-ing
know-ledge
knuc-kle
La-bel
la-bour
lad-der
la-dle
la-dy
lan-cet
land-lord
land-mark
land-scape
lan-guage
lan-guid
lar-der
lath-er
laugh-ter
law-ful
law-yer
lead-en
lead-er
lea-ky
lean-ness
learn-ing

leath-er	mam-mon	mock-er	na-vy
length-en	man-gle	mod-el	neat-ness
lev-el	man-ly	mod-ern	need-ful
le″-vy	man-ner	mod-est	nee-dle
li-bel	man-tle	mois-ture	ne-gro
li-cense	ma-ny	mo-ment	neigh-bour
life-less	mar-ble	mon-key	nei-ther
light-ning	marks-man	mon-ster	ne″-phew
lim-it	mar-row	month-ly	ner-vous
lin-quist	mar-shal	mor-al	net-tle
li-on	mar-tyr	mor-tar	new-ly
lit-ter	ma-son	most-ly	new-ness
lit-tle	mas-ter	moth-er	night-cap
live-ly	mat-ter	mo-tive	nim-ble
liv-er	max-im	move-ment	no-ble
liz-ard	may-or	moun-tain	non-sense
lead-ing	mea-ly	mourn-ful	nos-tril
lob-by	mean-ing	mouth-ful	noth-ing
lob-ster	mea-sure	mud-dle	no-tice
lock-et	med-dle	mud-dy	nov-el
lo-cust	meek-ness	muf-fle	num-ber
lodg-er	mem-ber	mum-ble	nurs-er
lof-ty	mend-er	mur-der	nur-ture
long-ing	men-tal	mur-mur	Oak-en
loose-ness	mer-chant	mush-room	oat-meal
lord-ly	mer-cy	mu-sic	ob-ject
loud-ness	mer-it	mus-lin	ob-long
love-ly	mes-sage	mus-tard	o-dour
lov-er	met-al	mus-ty	of-fer
low-ly	meth-od	mut-ton	of-fice
low-ness	mid-dle	muz-zle	oil-man
loy-al	migh-ty	myr-tle	oint-ment
lug-gage	mild-ness	Nail-er	old-er
lum-ber	mill-stone	na-ked	ol-ive
lurk-er	mil-ky	name-less	o-men
luc-ky	mil-ler	nap-kin	on-set
Mag-got	mind-ful	nar-row	o-pen
ma-jor	mis-chief	na-tive	or-ange
ma-ker	mi-ser	na-ture	or-der
mal-let	mix-ture	naugh-ty	or-gan

oth-er	pelt-ing	plu-mage	prod-uct
o-ver	pen-man	plum-met	prof-it
out-cry	pen-ny	plump-ness	prog-ress
out-most	peo-ple	plun-der	pro"-ject
out-rage	pep-per	plu-ral	prom-ise
out-work	per-fect	poach-er	proph-et
own-er	per-il	pock-et	pros-per
oys-ter	per-ish	po-et	proud-ly
Pack-age	per-jure	poi-son	pry-ing
pack-et	per-son	po-ker	pru-dence
pad-dle	pes-tle	po-lar	psalm-ist
pad-lock	pet-ty	pol-ish	pub-lic
pain-ful	pew-ter	pom-pous	pub-lish
pain-ter	phi-al	pop-py	pud-ding
pal-ace	phys-ic	post-age	pud-dle
pale-ness	pic-kle	pos-ture	pul-pit
pam-phlet	pic-ture	po-tent	pump-er
pan-cake	pie-ces	poul-try	pun-ish
pan-ic	pil-fer	poun-der	pup-py
pan-try	pil-grim	pow-er	pure-ness
pa-per	pill-box	pow-der	pur-pose
par-cel	pi-lot	prac-tice	pu-trid
parch-ment	pim-ple	prais-er	puz-zle
par-don	pin-cers	prat-tle	Quad-rant
pa-rent	pinch-ing	pray-er	quag-mire
par-lour	pi-per	preach-er	quar-rell
par-rot	pip-pin	pre-cept	quar-ry
part-ner	pi-rate	pref-ace	quar-ter
par-ty	pitch-er	prel-ude	queer-ly
pas-sage	pi"-ty	pres-ence	quick-ly
pass-port	pla-ces	pres-ent	quick-sand
pas-ture	plain-tiff	press-er	qui-et
pat-ent	plan-et	pric-kle	qui-ver
pave-ment	plant-er	priest-hood	Rab-bit
pay-ment	plas-ter	prim-er	rab-ble
pea-cock	plat-ter	prin-cess	ra-cer
peb-ble	play-er	pri-vate	rad-ish
ped-lar	pleas-ant	prob-lem	raf-ter
peep-er	pleas-ure	proc-tor	rag-ged
pee-vish	plot-ter	pro-duce	rail-er

rai-ment	ri-der	Sab-bath	see-ing
rain-bow	ri-fle	sa-ble	sell-er
rai-ny	right-ful	sa-bre	sen-ate
rais-er	rig-our	sack-cloth	sense-less
rai-sin	ri-ot	sad-dle	sen-tence
ral-ly	rip-ple	safe-ly	se-quel
ram-ble	ri-val	safe-ty	ser-mon
ram-part	riv-er	saf-fron	ser-pent
ran-dom	riv-et	sail-or	ser-vant
ran-ger	roar-ing	sal-ad	ser-vice
ran-kle	rob-ber	sal-mon	set-ter
ran-sack	roc-ket	salt-ish	set-tle
ran-som	roll-er	sal-vage	shab-by
rant-er	ro-man	sam-ple	shack-le
rap-id	roo-my	san-dal	shad-ow
rap-ine	ro-sy	san-dy	shal-low
rap-ture	rot-ten	san-guine	shame-ful
rash-ness	round-ish	sap-ling	shame-less
rath-er	ro-ver	satch-el	shape-less
rat-tle	roy-al	sat-in	shar-pen
rav-age	rub-ber	sav-age	sharp-er
ra-ven	rub-bish	sau-cer	shear-ing
raw-ness	ru-by	sau-sage	shel-ter
ra-zor	rud-der	saw-yer	shep-herd
rea-der	rude-ness	say-ing	sher-iff
rea-dy	rue-ful	scaf-fold	shil-ling
re-al	ruf-fle	scan-dal	shin-ing
reap-er	rug-ged	scar-let	ship-wreck
rea-son	ru-in	scat-ter	shock-ing
reb-el	rul-er	schol-ar	short-er
re-cent	rum-ble	sci-ence	shov-el
reck-on	rum-mage	scorn-ful	should-er
rec-tor	ru-mour	scrip-ture	show-er
ref-use	rum-ple	scru-ple	shuf-fle
rent-al	run-let	scuf-fle	shut-ter
rest-less	run-ning	scull-er	sick-en
rev-el	rup-ture	sculp-ture	sick-ness
rib-and	rus-tic	seam-less	sight-less
rich-es	rus-ty	sea-son	sig-nal
rid-dle	ruth-less	se-cret	si-lence

si-lent	spee-dy	stur-dy	tam-per
sim-ple	spin-dle	sub-ject	tan-gle
sin-ew	spin-ner	suc-cour	ta-per
sin-ful	spir-it	suck-ling	tar-dy
sing-ing	spite-ful	sud-den	tar-get
sing-er	splint-er	suf-fer	taste-less
sin-gle	spo-ken	sul-len	tas-ter
sin-ner	sport-ing	sul-tan	tat-tle
sis-ter	spot-less	sul-try	taw-dry
sit-ting	sprin-kle	sum-mer	taw-ny
skil-ful	spun-gy	sum-mit	tai-lor
slack-en	squan-der	sum-mons	tell-er
slan-der	squeam-ish	sun-day	tem-per
slav-ish	sta-ble	sup-per	tem-pest
sleep-er	stag-ger	sup-ple	tem-ple
slee-py	sta-ple	sure-ty	tempt-er
slip-per	star-tle	sur-feit	ten-ant
slop-py	state-ly	sur-ly	ten-der
sloth-ful	sta″-tue	sur-name	ter-race
slug-gard	stat-ure	sur-plice	ter-ror
slum-ber	stead-fast	swag-ger	thank-ful
smell-ing	stee-ple	swal-low	thatch-er
smug-gle	steer-age	swar-thy	thaw-ing
snap-per	stiff-en	swear-ing	there-fore
sneak-ing	sti-fle	swea″-ty	thick-et
snuf-fle	still-ness	sweep-ing	thiev-ish
sock-et	stin-gy	sweet-en	thim-ble
soft-en	stir-rup	sweet-ness	think-ing
sol-ace	stom-ach	swell-ing	thirs-ty
sol-emn	sto-ny	swift-ness	thor-ny
sol-id	stor-my	swim-ming	thorn-back
sor-did	sto-ry	sys-tem	thought-ful
sor-row	stout-ness	Tab-by	thou-sand
sor-ry	strict-ly	ta-ble	thrash-er
sot-tish	stri-king	tac-kle	threat-en
sound-ness	strip-ling	ta-ker	throb-bing
spar-kle	struc-ture	tal-ent	thump-ing
spar-row	stub-born	tal-low	thun-der
speak-er	stu-dent	tal-ly	thurs-day
speech-less	stum-ble	tame-ly	tick-et

tic-kle	troop-er	Va-cant	want-ing
ti-dy	tro-phy	va-grant	war-fare
tight-en	trou″-ble	vain-ly	war-like
tim-ber	trow-sers	val-ley	war-rant
time-ly	tru-ant	van-ish	wash-ing
tinc-ture	tru-ly	van-quish	wa-ter
tin-der	trum-pet	var-nish	watch-ful
tin-ker	trun-dle	va-ry	wa-ver
tin-sel	trus-ty	vel-vet	weak-en
tip-pet	tues-day	ven-om	wea-ry
tire-some	tu-lip	ven-ture	weal-thy
ti-tle	tum-ble	ver-dant	wea-pon
toi-let	tu-mour	ver-dict	wea-ther
to-ken	tu-mult	ver-ger	weep-ing
tor-ment	tun-nel	ver-juice	weigh-ty
tor-rent	tur-ban	ver-min	wel-fare
tor-ture	tur-bid	ve″-ry	wheat-en
to-tal	tur-key	ves-per	whis-per
tot-ter	turn-er	ves-try	whis-tle
tow-el	tur-nip	vex-ed	whole-some
tow-er	turn-stile	vic-ar	wick-ed
tra-ding	tur-ret	vic-tor	wid-ow
traf-fic	tur-tle	vig-our	will-ing
trai-tor	tu-tor	vil-lain	win-ter
tram-mel	twi-light	vi-per	wis-dom
tram-ple	twin-kle	vir-gin	wit-ness
trans-fer	twit-ter	vir-tue	wit-ty
trea-cle	ty-rant	vis-age	wo-ful
trea-son	Um-pire	vis-it	won-der
treas-ure	un-cle	vo-cal	wor-ship
trea-tise	un-der	voy-age	Year-ly
treat-ment	up-per	vul-gar	yel-low
trea-ty	up-right	vul-ture	yon-der
trem-ble	up-shot	Wa-fer	young-er
tres-pass	up-ward	wag-tail	youth-ful
tri-fle	ur-gent	wait-er	Za-ny
trim-mer	use-ful	wake-ful	zeal-ous
tri″-ple	ush-er	walk-er	zen-ith
trip-ping	ut-most	wal-nut	ze″-phyr
tri-umph	ut-ter	wan-der	zig-zag

*Entertaining and Instructive Lessons, in Words not
exceeding* TWO *Syllables.*

Lesson I.

I want my din-ner; I want pud-ding. It is not
rea-dy yet; it will be rea-dy soon, then Thom-as
shall have his din-ner. Lay the cloth. Where are
the knives, and forks, and plates? The clock strikes
one; take up the din-ner. May I have some meat?

No: you shall have som-thing ni-cer. Here is some
ap-ple dump-ling for you; and here are some pease,
and some beans, and car-rots, and turnips, and rice-
pud-ding, and bread.

Lesson 2.

There was a lit-tle boy, who was not high-er than
the ta-ble, and his pa-pa and mam-ma sent him to
school. It was a very pleas-ant morn-ing; the sun
shone, and the birds sung on the trees. Now this lit-
tle boy did not love his book much, for he was but a
sil-ly little boy, as I said before. If he had been a

big boy, I sup-pose he would have been wi-ser; but he had a great mind to play in-stead of go-ing to school. And he saw a bee fly-ing about, first up-on one flow-er and then up-on an-oth-er; so he said, Pret-ty Bee! will you come and play with me? But the bee said, No, I must not be i-dle, I must go and ga-ther hon-ey.

Lesson 3.

Then the i-dle boy met a dog; and he said, Dog! will you play with me? But the dog said, No, I must not be i-dle, I am go-ing to watch my master's house. I must make haste for fear bad men may get in. Then the lit-tle boy went to a hay-rick, and he saw a bird pull-ing some hay out of the hay-rick, and he said, Bird! will you come and play with me? But the bird said, No, I must not be i-dle, I must get some hay to build my nest with, and some moss and some wool. So the bird flew away.

Lesson 4.

Then the i-dle boy saw a horse; and he said, Horse! will you play with me? But the horse said, No, I must not be i-dle; I must go and plough, or else there will be no corn to make bread of. Then the lit-tle boy thought to him-self, What, is no-bo-dy idle? then lit-tle boys must not be i-dle ei-ther. So he made haste, and went to school, and learn-ed his les-son ve-ry well, and the mas-ter said he was a ve-ry good boy.

Lesson 5.

Thom-as, what a clev-er thing it is to read! A lit-tle while a-go, you know, you could on-ly read lit-tle words; and you were forced to spell them c-a-t, cat: d-o-g, dog. Now you can read pret-ty sto-ries, and I am go-ing to tell you some.

I will tell you a sto-ry a-bout a lamb. There was a kind shep-herd, who had a great ma-ny sheep and lambs. He took a great deal of care of them; and gave them sweet fresh grass to eat, and clear wa-ter to drink; and if they were sick, he was ve-ry good to them: and when they climb-ed up a steep hill, and the lambs were tired, he u-sed to car-ry them in his arms; and when they were all eat-ing their sup-pers in the field, he u-sed to sit up-on a stile, and play them a tune, and sing to them; and so they were hap-py sheep and lambs. And every night this shep-herd u-sed to pen them up in a fold, to keep them in safe-ty from the gree-dy wolf.

Lesson 6.

Now they were all ve-ry hap-py, as I told you, and lov-ed the shep-herd dear-ly, that was so good to them, all except one fool-ish lit-tle lamb. And this fool-ish lamb did not like to be shut up at night in the fold; and she came to her moth-er, who was a wise old sheep, and said to her, I won-der why we are shut up so all night! the dogs are not shut up, and why should we be shut up? I think it is ve-ry hard, and I will get a-way if I can, that I will, for I like to run a-bout where I please, and I think it is very pleasant in the woods by moonlight. Then the old sheep said to her, You are very sil-ly, you lit-tle

lamb, you had bet-ter stay in the fold. The shep-
herd is so good to us, that we should al-ways do as
he bids us; and if you wan-der a-bout by your-self, I
dare say you will come to some harm. I dare say
not, said the lit-tle lamb.

Lesson 7.

And so when the night came, and the shep-herd
call-ed them all to come in-to the fold, she would not
come, but hid her-self; and when the rest of the
lambs were all in the fold, and fast a-sleep, she came
out, and jump-ed, and frisk-ed, and dan-ced about;
and she got out of the field, and got in-to a forest full
of trees, and a very fierce wolf came rush-ing out of
a cave, and howl-ed very loud. Then the sil-ly lamb
wish-ed she had been shut up in the fold; but the
fold was a great way off; and the wolf saw her, and
seiz-ed her, and car-ried her away to a dis-mal dark
den, spread all o-ver with bones and blood; and there
the wolf had two cubs, and the wolf said to them,
"Here I have brought you a young fat lamb;" and
so the cubs took her and growl-ed over her a lit-tle
while, and then tore her to pie-ces and ate her up.

Lesson 8.

There was once a lit-tle boy, who was a sad
cow-ard. He was walk-ing by himself one day,
and a pret-ty black dog came out of a house,
and said, Bow-wow, bow-wow; and came to the
lit-tle boy, and jump-ed up-on him, and want-ed
to play with him, but the lit-tle boy ran away. The
dog ran af-ter him, and cri-ed loud-er, Bow, wow,
wow; but he only meant to say, Good morning, how
do you do? but this lit-tle boy was sad-ly a-fraid, and
ran a-way as fast as he could, with-out look-ing before him; and he tum-bled into a very dir-ty ditch,
and there he lay crying at the bot-tom of the ditch,

for he could not get out: and I be-lieve he would
have lain there all day, but the dog was so good,
that he went to the house where the lit-tle boy lived,
on purpose to tell them where he was. So, when he
came to the house, he scratch-ed at the door, and
said, Bow-wow; for he could not speak a-ny plainer.
So they came to the door, and said, What do you
want, you black dog. We do not know you. Then
the dog went to Ralph the servant, and pull-ed him
by the coat, and pull-ed him till he brought him to
the ditch, and the dog and Ralph be-tween them got
the lit-tle boy out of the ditch; but he was all over
mud, and quite wet, and all the folks laugh-ed at him
be-cause he was a cow-ard.

Lesson 9.

One day, in the month of June, Thomas had got all his things ready to set out on a little jaunt of pleasure with a few of his friends, but the sky became black with thick clouds, and on that account he was forced to wait some time in suspense. Being at last stopped by a heavy shower of rain, he was so vexed, that he could not refrain from tears; and sitting down in a sulky humour, would not suffer any one to comfort him.

Towards night the clouds began to vanish; the sun shone with great brightness, and the whole face of nature seemed to be changed. Robert then took Thomas with him into the fields, and the freshness of the air, the music of the birds, and the greenness of the grass, filled him with pleasure. "Do you see," said Robert, "what a change has taken place? Last night the ground was parched; the flowers, and all the things seemed to droop. To what cause must we impute this happy change?" Struck with the folly of his own conduct in the morning, Thomas was forced to admit, that the useful rain which fell that morning, had done all this good,

Words of TWO *Syllables, accented on the* SECOND.

Ab-hor	a-mend	a-ware	com-mand
a-bove	a-mong	a-wry	com-mend
a-bout	a-muse	Bap-tize	com-ment
ab-surd	an-noy	be-cause	com-mit
ac-cept	ap-peal	be-come	com-mune
ac-count	ap-pear	be-fore	com-mute
ac-cuse	ap-plaud	be-head	com-pact
ac-quaint	ap-ply	be-hold	com-pare
ac-quire	ap-point	be-lieve	com-pel
ac-quit	ap-proach	be-neath	com-pile
ad-here	ap-prove	be-numb	com-plain
ad-just	a-rise	be-seech	com-plete
ad-mit	ar-rest	be-seem	com-ply
a-dorn	as-cend	be-set	com-pose
ad-vice	as-cent	be-sides	com-pound
ad-vise	a-shore	be-siege	com-press
a-far	a-side	be-smear	com-prise
af-fair	as-sault	be-smoke	com-pute
af-fix	as-sert	be-speak	con-ceal
af-flict	as-sist	be-stow	con-cede
a-fraid	as-sume	be-tide	con-ceit
a-gain	as-sure	be-times	con-ceive
a-gainst	a-stray	be-tray	con-cern
ag-gress	a-stride	be-tween	con-cert
a-go	a-tone	be-wail	con-cise
a-larm	at-tend	be-ware	con-clude
a-las	at-test	be-yond	con-coct
a-lert	at-tire	block-ade	con-demn
a-like	at-tract	bom-bard	con-dense
a-live	a-vail	Ca-nal	con-dole
al-lege	a-vast	car-bine	con-duce
al-lude	a-venge	ca-ress	con-duct
al-lure	a-verse	car-mine	con-fer
al-ly	a-vert	ce-ment	con-fess
a-loft	a-void	cock-ade	con-fide
a-lone	a-vow	co-here	con-fine
a-long	a-wait	col-lect	con-firm
a-loof	a-wake	com-bine	con-form

con-found	de-ceive	de-scribe	dis-mount
con-front	de-cide	de-sert	dis-own
con-fuse	de-claim	de-serve	dis-pel
con-fute	de-clare	de-sign	dis-pense
con-join	de-cline	de-sire	dis-perse
con-joint	de-coy	de-sist	dis-place
con-nect	de-cree	de-spair	dis-play
con-sent	de-cry	de-spise	dis-please
con-serve	de-duct	de-spoil	dis-port
con-sign	de-face	de-spond	dis-pose
con-sist	de-fame	de-stroy	dis-praise
con-sole	de-feat	de-tain	dis-solve
con-sort	de-fect	de-tect	dis-til
con-spire	de-fence	de-ter	dis-tinct
con-strain	de-fer	de-test	dis-tort
con-struct	de-fine	de-vise	dis-tract
con-sult	de-form	de-volve	dis-tress
con-sume	de-fraud	de-vote	dis-trust
con-tain	de-grade	de-vour	dis-turb
con-tempt	de-gree	de-vout	dis-use
con-tend	de-ject	dif-fuse	di-verge
con-tent	de-lay	di-gest	di-vert
con-test	de-light	di-late	di-vest
con-tract	de-lude	di-lute	di-vide
con-trast	de-mand	di-rect	di-vine
con-trol	de-mean	dis-arm	di-vorce
con-vene	de-note	dis-cern	di-vulge
con-vert	de-ny	dis-charge	dra-gon
con-vey	de-part	dis-claim	E-clipse
con-vict	de-pend	dis-close	ef-face
con-vince	de-pict	dis-course	ef-fect
con-voke	de-plore	dis-cuss	e-ject
con-vulse	de-pose	dis-dain	e-lapse
cor-rect	de-prave	dis-ease	e-late
cur-tail	de-press	dis-grace	e-lect
De-bar	de-prive	dis-guise	e-lude
de-base	de-pute	dis-gust	el-lipse
de-bate	de-ride	dis-like	em-bark
de-cay	de-scant	dis-may	em-brace
de-ceit	de-scend	dis-miss	em-ploy

en-act	ex-cel	for-bid	in-crease
en-close	ex-cept	fore-bode	in-cur
en-dear	ex-cess	fore-doom	in-deed
en-dite	ex-change	fore-go	in-dent
en-dorse	ex-cise	fore-know	in-duce
en-due	ex-cite	fore-see	in-dulge
en-dure	ex-claim	fore-stall	in-fect
en-force	ex-clude	fore-tell	in-fer
en-gage	ex-cuse	fore-warn	in-fest
en-grave	ex-empt	for-give	in-firm
en-hance	ex-ert	for-lorn	in-flame
en-join	ex-haust	for-sake	in-flate
en-joy	ex-ist	for-swear	in-flict
en-large	ex-pand	forth-with	in-form
en-rage	ex-pect	ful-fil	in-ject
en-rich	ex-pend	Ga-zette	in-list
en-rol	ex-pense	gen-teel	in-quire
en-slave	ex-pert	grim-ace	in-sane
en-sure	ex-pire	Im-bibe	in-sert
en-tail	ex-plain	im-mense	in-sist
en-throne	ex-plode	im-merse	in-snare
en-tice	ex-ploit	im-pair	in-spect
en-tire	ex-plore	im-part	in-spire
en-treat	ex-port	im-peach	in-stall
en-twine	ex-pose	im-pede	in-stil
e-quip	ex-press	im-pel	in-struct
e-rase	ex-tend	im-pend	in-sult
e-rect	ex-tent	im-plant	in-tend
e-scape	ex-tinct	im-plore	in-tense
es-cort	ex-tol	im-ply	in-ter
e-spy	ex-tort	im-port	in-thral
e-state	ex-tract	im-pose	in-trigue
e-steem	ex-treme	im-press	in-trude
e-vade	ex-ude	im-print	in-trust
e-vent	ex-ult	im-prove	in-vade
e-vict	Fa-tigue	im-pure	in-vent
e-vince	fer-ment	im-pute	in-vert
e-voke	fif-teen	in-cite	in-vest
ex-act	fo-ment	in-cline	in-vite
ex-ceed	for-bear	in-clude	in-voke

in-volve	oc-cur	pre-fer	pur-vey
in-ure	of-fend	pre-fix	Re-bel
Ja-pan	op-pose	pre-judge	re-bound
jo-cose	op-press	pre-pare	re-buff
La-ment	or-dain	pre-sage	re-build
lam-poon	out-bid	pre-scribe	re-buke
Ma-chine	out-brave	pre-sent	re-call
main-tain	out-do	pre-serve	re-cant
ma-nure	out-grow	pre-side	re-cede
ma-rine	out-leap	pre-sume	re-ceipt
ma-ture	out-live	pre-tence	re-ceive
mis-cast	out-right	pre-tend	re-cess
mis-chance	out-run	pre-text	re-cite
mis-deed	out-sail	pre-vail	re-claim
mis-give	out-shine	pre-vent	re-cline
mis-hap	out-strip	pro-ceed	re-cluse
mis-judge	out-walk	pro-claim	re-cord
mis-lay	out-weigh	pro-cure	re-count
mis-lead	Pa-rade	pro-duce	re-course
mis-name	pa-role	pro-fess	re-cruit
mis-place	par-take	pro-found	re-cur
mis-print	pa-trol	pro-fuse	re-deem
mis-quote	per-form	pro-ject	re-doubt
mis-rule	per-fume	pro-lix	re-dress
mis-take	per-haps	pro-long	re-duce
mis-trust	per-mit	pro-mote	re-fect
mis-use	per-plex	pro-nounce	re-fer
mo-lest	per-sist	pro-pel	re-fine
mo-rose	per-spire	pro-pose	re-fit
Neg-lect	per-suade	pro-pound	re-flect
O-bey	per-tain	pro-rogue	re-flow
ob-ject	per-vade	pro-tect	re-form
o-blige	per-verse	pro-test	re-tract
ob-lique	per-vert	pro-tract	re-frain
ob-scure	pla-card	pro-trude	re-fresh
ob-serve	pos-sess	pro-vide	re-fund
ob-struct	post-pone	pro-voke	re-fuse
ob-tain	pre-cede	pur-loin	re-fute
ob-trude	pre-clude	pur-sue	re-gain
ob-tuse	pre-dict	pur-suit	re-gale

re-gard	re-print	sub-mit	un-close
re-gret	re-proach	sub-side	un-couth
re-hear	re-proof	sub-sist	un-do
re-ject	re-prove	sub-tract	un-done
re-joice	re-pulse	sub-vert	un-dress
re-join	re-pute	suc-ceed	un-fair
re-lapse	re-quest	suf-fice	un-fed
re-late	re-quire	sug-gest	un-fit
re-lax	re-quite	sup-ply	un-fold
re-lay	re-seat	sup-port	un-gird
re-lease	re-serve	sup-pose	un-glue
re-lent	re-sign	sup-press	un-hinge
re-lief	re-sist	sur-round	un-hook
re-lieve	re-solve	sur-vey	un-horse
re-light	re-spect	sus-pend	un-hurt
re-ly	re-store	sus-pense	u-nite
re-main	re-tain	There-of	un-just
re-mand	re-tard	tor-ment	un-knit
re-mark	re-tire	tra-duce	un-known
re-mind	re-treat	trans-act	un-lace
re-miss	re-turn	tran-scend	un-lade
re-mote	re-venge	trans-fer	un-like
re-move	re-vere	trans-form	un-load
re-mount	re-vile	trans-late	un-lock
re-new	re-volt	trans-mit	un-loose
re-nown	re-volve	trans-pire	un-mask
re-pair	re-ward	trans-plant	un-paid
re-past	ro-mance	trans-pose	un-ripe
re-pay	Sa-lute	trus-tee	un-safe
re-peal	se-clude	Un-apt	un-seen
re-peat	se-cure	un-bar	un-sound
re-pel	se-date	un-bend	un-spent
re-pent	se-duce	un-bind	un-true
re-pine	se-lect	un-blest	un-wise
re-place	se-rene	un-bolt	up-hold
re-ply	se-vere	un-born	With-draw
re-port	sin-cere	un-bought	with-hold
re-pose	sub-due	un-bound	with-in
re-press	sub-join	un-chain	with-out
re-prieve	sub-lime	un-clasp	Your-self.

Entertaining and Instructive Lessons, in Words not exceeding THREE *Syllables.*

Lesson 1.

Gold is of a deep yellow colour. It is very pretty and bright. It is a great deal heav-i· er than any thing else. Men dig it out of the ground. Shall I take my spade and get some? No, there is none in this country. It comes from a great way off; and it lies deeper a great deal than you could dig with your spade. Sov-er-eigns are made of gold; and so are half-sov-er-eigns, and watches sometimes.

Lesson 2.

Silver is white and shining. Spoons are made of silver, and waiters, and crowns, and half-crowns, and shillings, and six-pen-ces. Silver comes from a great way off; from Peru and Mexico.

Copper is red. The kettles and pots are made of copper; and brass is made of copper. Brass is bright and yellow, almost like gold. The sauce-pans are made of brass; and the locks upon the door, and the can-dle-sticks. What is that green upon the sauce-pan? It is rusty; the green is called ver-di-gris; it would kill you if you were to eat it.

Lesson 3.

Iron is very hard. It is not pretty; but I do not know what we should do without it, for it makes us a great many things. The tongs, and the poker, and shovel, are made of iron. Go and ask Dobbin if he can plough without the plough-share? Well, what does he say? He says, No, he cannot. But the plough-share is made of iron. Will iron melt in the fire? Put the poker in and try. Well, is it melted? No, but it is red-hot, and soft; it will bend. But I will tell you, Charles; iron will melt in a very, very hot fire, when it has been in a great while; then it will melt.

Come, let us go to the smith's shop. What is he doing? He has a forge; he blows the fire with a great pair of bellows to make the iron hot. Now it is hot. Now he takes it out with the tongs, and puts it upon the anvil. Now he beats it with a hammer. How hard he works! The sparks fly about: pretty bright sparks! What is the blacksmith making? He is making nails, and horse-shoes, and a great many things.

Lesson 4.

Steel is made of iron. Steel is very bright and hard. Knives and scissors are made of steel.

Lead is soft and very heavy. Here is a piece : lift it. There is lead in the casement; and the spout is lead, and the cistern is lead, and bullets are made of lead.

Tin is white and soft. Is is bright too. The dripping-pan and the re-flect-or are all cov-er-ed with tin.

Quick-sil-ver is very bright, like silver ; and it is very heavy. See how it runs about! You cannot catch it. You cannot pick it up. There is quick-sil-ver in the weath-er-glass.

Gold, silver, copper, iron, lead, tin, quick-sil-ver ; one, two, three, four, five, six, seven metals. They are all dug out of the ground.

Lesson 5.

There was a little boy whose name was Harry, and his papa and mamma sent him to school. Now Harry was a clever fellow, and loved his book ; and he got to be first in his class. So his mamma got up one morning very early, and called Betty the maid, and said, Betty, I think we must make a cake for Harry, for he has learned his book very well. And Betty said, Yes, will all my heart. So they made him a nice cake. It was very large, and stuffed full of plums and sweetmeats, orange and citron; and it was iced all over with sugar : it was white and smooth on the top like snow. So this cake was sent to the school. When little Harry saw it he was very glad, and jumped about for joy, and he hardly staid for a knife to cut a piece, but gnawed it with his teeth. So

he eat till the bell rang for school, and after school he
eat again, and eat till he went to bed; nay, he laid
his cake under his pillow, and sat up in the night to
eat some.

He ate till it was all gone.—But soon after, this
lit-tle boy was very sick, and ev-e-ry body said, I
won-der what is the matter wilh Harry: he used to
be brisk, and play about more nimbly than any or
the boys; and now he looks pale and is very ill.
And some-bo-dy said, Harry has had a rich cake, and
eaten it all up very soon, and that has made him ill.
So they sent for Doctor Rhubarb, and he gave him I
do not know how much bitter physic. Poor Harry
did not like it at all, but he was forced to take it, or
else he would have died, you know. So at last he
got well again, but his mamma said she would send
him no more cakes.

Lesson 6.

Now there was an-oth-er boy, who was one of
Harry's school-fel-lows; his name was Peter; the
boys used to call him Peter Careful. And Peter had
written his mamma a very clean pretty letter; there
was not one blot in it all. So his mamma sent him
a cake. Now Peter thought with himself, I will not
make myself sick with this good cake, as silly Harry
did; I will keep it a great while. So he took the
cake, and tugged it up stairs. It was very heavy; he
could hardly carry it. And he locked it up in his
box, and once a-day he crept slily up stairs and ate a
very little piece, and then locked his box again. So

he kept it sev-er-al weeks and it was not gone, for it was very large; but behold! the mice got into the box and nibbled some. And the cake grew dry and mouldy, and at last was good for nothing at all. So he was o-bli-ged to throw it away, and it grieved him to the very heart.

Lesson 7.

Well; there was an-oth-er lit-tle boy at the same school, whose name was Richard. And one day his mamma sent him a cake, because she loved him dearly, and he loved her dearly. So when the cake came, Richard said to his school-fel-lows, I have got a cake, come let us go and eat it. So they came about him like a parcel of bees; and Richard took a slice of cake himself, and then gave a piece to one, and a piece to an-oth-er, and a piece to an-oth-er, till it was almost gone. Then Richard put the rest by, and said, I will eat it to-morrow.

He then went to play, and the boys all played to-geth-er mer-ri-ly. But soon after an old blind Fiddler came into the court; he had a long white beard; and because he was blind, he had a little dog in a string to lead him. So he came into the court, and sat down upon a stone, and said, My pretty lads, if you will, I will play you a tune. And they all left off their sport, and came and stood round him.

And Richard saw that while he played the tears ran down his cheeks. And Richard said, Old man, why do you cry? And the old man said, Because I am very hungry: I have no-bo-dy to give me any dinner or supper: I have nothing in the world but this little dog: and I cannot work. If I could work I would. Then Richard went, without saying a word, and fetched the rest of his cake, which he had in-tend-ed to have eaten an-oth-er day, and he said, Here, old man, here is some cake for you.

The old man said, Where is it? for I am blind, I cannot see it. So Richard put it into his hat. And the Fiddler thanked him, and Richard was more glad than if he had eaten ten cakes.

Pray which do you love best? Do you love Harry best, or Peter best, or Richard best?

Lesson 8.

The noblest em-ploy-ment of the mind of man is to study the works of his Cre-a-tor. To him whom the science of nature de-light-eth, ev-e-ry object bringeth a proof of his God. His mind is lifted up

to heaven every moment, and his life shews what
i-de-a he en-ter-tains of e-ter-nal wisdom. If he
cast his eyes towards the clouds, will he not find the
heavens full of its wonders? If he look down on
the earth, doth not the worm proclaim to him, " Less
than in-fi-nite power could not have formed me?"

While the planets pursue their courses; while the
sun re-main-eth in his place; while the comet wan-
der-eth through space, and re-turn-eth to its des-tin-
ed spot again; who but God could have formed
them? Behold how awful their splendour! yet they
do not di-min-ish; lo, how rapid their motion! yet
one run-neth not in the way of an-oth-er. Look
down upon the earth, and see its produce; ex-am-ine
its bowels, and behold what they contain: have not
wisdom and power or-dain-ed the whole? Who bid-
deth the grass to spring up? who wa-ter-eth it at due
seasons? Behold the ox croppeth it; the horse and
the sheep, do they not feed upon it? Who is he that
pro-vi-deth for them, but the Lord?

Ab-di-cate
ab-ro-gate
ab-so-lute
ac-ci-dent
ac-cu-rate
ac-tu-ate
ad-ju-tant
ad-mi-ral
ad-vo-cate
af-fa-ble
ag-o-ny
al-der-man
a-li-en
am-nes-ty
an-ar-chy
an-ces-tor
an-i-mal
an-i-mate
an-nu-al
ap-pe-tite
ar-gu-ment
ar-mo-ry
ar-ro-gant
at-tri-bute
av-a-rice
au-di-tor
au-thor-ize
Ba″-che-lor
back-sli-der
back-ward-ness
ban-ish-ment
bar-ba-rous
bar-ren-ness
bar-ris-ter
bash-ful-ness
bat-tle-ment
beau-ti-ful
ben-e-fice

ben-e-fit
big-o-try
blood-suck-er
blun-der-buss
blun-der-er
blun-der-ing
blus-ter-er
bois-ter-ous
book-bind-er
bor-row-er
bot-tom-less
boun-ti-ful
broth-er-ly
bur-den-some
bur-gla-ry
bu-ri-al
Cab-i-net
cal-cu-late
cal-en-dar
cap-i-tal
cap-ti-vate
car-di-nal
care-ful-ly
car-pen-ter
cas-u-al
cat-a-logue
cat-e-chise
cat-e-chism
cel-e-brate
cen-tu-ry
cer-ti-fy
cham-ber-maid
cham-pi-on
char-ac-ter
char-i-ty
chas-tise-ment
chiv-al-ry
chem-i-cal

chem-is-try
cin-na-mon
cir-cu-late
cir-cum-spect
cir-cum-stance
clam-or-ous
clas-si-cal
clean-li-ness
col-o-ny
com-e-dy
com-fort-less
com-i-cal
com-pa-ny
com-pe-tent
com-ple-ment
com-pli-ment
com-pro-mise
con-fer-ence
con-fi-dence
con-flu-ence
con-gru-ous
con-ju-gal
con-que-ror
con-se-crate
con-se-quence
con-so-nant
con-sta-ble
con-stan-cy
con-sti-tute
con-ti-nence
con-tra-ry
con-ver-sant
co-pi-ous
cor-di-al
cor-mo-rant
cor-o-ner
cor-po-ral
cor-pu-lent

cos-tive-ness
cost-li-ness
cov-e-nant
cov-er-ing
cov-et-ous
coun-sel-lor
coun-te-nance
coun-ter-feit
coun-ter-pane
cour-te-ous
court-li-ness
cow-ard-ice
craft-i-ness
cred-i-ble
cred-i-tor
crim-i-nal
crit-i-cal
croc-o-dile
crook-ed-ness
cru-ci-fy
cru-el-ty
crus-ti-ness
cu-cum-ber
cul-pa-ble
cul-ti-vate
cu-ri-ous
cus-to-dy
cus-to-mer
Dan-ger-ous
de-cen-cy
ded-i-cate
del-i-cate
de-pu-ty
des-o-late
des-pe-rate
des-ti-ny
des-ti-tute
det-ri-ment
de-vi-ate
di-a-dem

di-a-logue
dil-i-gence
dis-ci-pline
dis-lo-cate
doc-u-ment
dow-a-ger
dra-pe-ry
du-ra-ble
Eb-o-ny
ed-i-tor
ed-u-cate
el-e-gant
el-e-ment
el-e-phant
el-e-vate
el-o-quence
em-i-nent
em-pe-ror
em-pha-sis
em-u-late
en-e-my
en-er-gy
en-ter-prise
es-ti-mate
ev-e-ry
ev-i-dent
ex-cel-lence
ex-cel-lent
ex-e-crate
ex-e-cute
ex-er-cise
ex-pi-ate
ex-qui-site
Fab-u-lous
fac-ul-ty
faith-ful-ly
fal-li-ble
fath-er-less
faul-ti-ly
fer-ven-cy

fes-ti-val
fe-ver-ish
fir-ma-ment
fish-e-ry
flat-te-ry
fool-ish-ness
fop-pe-ry
for-ti-fy
for-ward-ness
fraud-u-lent
free-hold-er
friv-o-lous
fro-ward-ly
fu-ner-al
fu-ri-ous
fur-ni-ture
Gain-say-er
gal-lant-ry
gal-le-ry
gar-de-ner
gar-ri-son
gau-di-ly
gen-er-al
gen-er-ous
gen-tle-man
gen-u-ine
gid-di-ness
gin-ger-bread
glim-mer-ing
glo-ri-fy
glut-ton-ous
god-li-ness
gor-man-dise
gov-ern-ment
gov-er-nor
grace-ful-ness
grad-u-ate
grate-ful-ly
grat-i-fy
grav-i-tate

greed-i-ness
griev-ous-ly
gun-pow-der
Hand-i-ly
hand-ker-chief
harm-less-ly
har-mo-ny
haugh-ti-ness
heav-i-ness
he"-rald-ry
he"-re-sy
he"-ri-tage
her-mit-age
hid-e-ous
hind-er-most
his-to-ry
hoa-ri-ness
ho-li-ness
hon-es-ty
hope-ful-ness
hos-pi-tal
hus-band-man
hyp-o-crite
Idle-ness
ig-no-rant
im-i-tate
im-ple-ment
im-pli-cate
im-po-tence
im-pu-dent
in-ci-dent
in-di-cate
in-di-gent
in-do-lent
in-dus-try
in-fa-my
in-fan-cy
in-fi-nite
in-flu-ence
in-ju-ry

in-ner-most
in-no-cence
in-so-lent
in-stant-ly
in-sti-tute
in-stru-ment
in-ter-course
in-ter-est
in-ter-val
in-ter-view
in-ti-mate
in-tri-cate
Joc-u-lar
jol-li-ness
jo-vi-al
jus-ti-fy
Kid-nap-per
kna-vish-ly
knot-ti-ly
La-bour-er
lar-ce-ny
leg-a-cy
len-i-ty
lep-ro-sy
leth-ar-gy
lib-er-al
lib-er-tine
like-li-hood
li-on-ess
lit-er-al
lof-ti-ness
low-li-ness
lu-na-cy
lu-na-tic
lux-u-ry
Mag-ni-fy
ma-jes-ty
main-te-nance
man-age-ment
man-ful-ly

man-li-ness
man-u-al
man-u-script
mar-i-gold
mar-i-ner
mar-row-bone
mas-cu-line
mel-low-ness
mel-o-dy
melt-ing-ly
mem-o-ry
men-di-cant
mer-can-tile
mer-chan-dise
mer-ci-ful
mer-ri-ment
min-er-al
min-is-ter
mir-a-cle
mis-chiev-ous
mod-er-ate
mon-u-ment
mourn-ful-ly
mul-ti-tude
mu-si-cal
mu-tu-al
mys-te-ry
Na-ked-ness
nar-ra-tive
nat-u-ral
neg-a-tive
night-in-gale
nom-i-nate
not-a-ble
no-ta-ry
no-ti-fy
nov-el-ist
nov-el-ty
nour-ish-ment
nu-mer-ous

nun-ne-ry
nur-se-ry
nu-tri-ment
Ob-du-rate
ob-lo-quy
ob-so-lete
ob-sta-cle
ob-sti-nate
ob-vi-ous
oc-cu-py
oc-u-list
o-di-ous
of-fer-ing
om-i-nous
op-er-ate
op-po-site
op-u-lent
or-a-cle
or-a-tor
or-der-ly
or-di-nance
or-gan-ist
or-i-gin
or-na-ment
or-tho-dox
o-ver-flow
o-ver-sight
out-ward-ly
Pa"-ci-fy
pa-pa-cy
par-a-dise .
par-a-dox
par-a-graph
par-a-pet
par-a-phrase
par-a-site
par-o-dy
pa-tri-arch
pa"-tron-age
peace-a-ble

pec-to-ral
pec-u-late
ped-an-try
pen-al-ty
pen-e-trate
pen-i-tence
pen-sive-ly
pen-u-ry
per-fect-ness
per-ju-ry
per-ma-nence
per-pe-trate
per-se-cute
per-son-age
per-ti-nence
pes-ti-lence
pet-ri-fy
phy-si-cal
pi-e-ty
pil-fer-er
pin-na-cle
plen-ti-ful
plun-der-er
po-e-try
pol-i-cy
pol-i-tic
pop-u-lar
pop-u-lous
pos-si-ble
po-ten-tate
pov-er-ty
prac-ti-cal
pre-am-ble
pre-ce-dent
pres-i-dent
prev-a-lent
prin-ci-pal
pris-on-er
priv-i-lege
prob-a-ble

prod-i-gy
prof-li-gate
pro"-per-ly
pro"-per-ty
pros-e-cute
pros-per-ous
prot-est-ant
prov-en-der
prov-i-dence
punc-tu-al
pun-ish-ment
pyr-a-mid
Qual-i-fy
quan-ti-ty
quar-rel-some
quer-u-lous
qui-et-ness
Rad-i-cal
rav-en-ous
re-cent-ly
re"-com-pence
rem-e-dy
ren-o-vate
re"-qui-site
re"-tro-grade
rev-e-rend
rhet-o-ric
right-e-ous
rit-u-al
riv-u-let
rob-be-ry
rot-ten-ness
roy-al-ty
Sac-ra-ment
sac-ri-fice
sal-a-ry
sanc-ti-fy
sat-ir-ist
sat-is-fy
sau-ci-ness

scrip-tu-ral
scru-pu-lous
se-cre-cy
sec-u-lar
sen-su-al
sep-a-rate
sev-er-al
sit-u-ate
slip-pe-ry
sor-ce-ry
spec-ta-cle
stig-ma-tize
strat-a-gem
straw-ber-ry
stren-u-ous
sub-se-quent
suc-cu-lent
suf-fo-cate
sum-ma-ry

sup-ple-ment
sus-te-nance
syc-a-more
sym-pa-thise
Tem-po-rize
ten-den-cy
ten-der-ness
tes-ta-ment
tit-u-lar
tol-er-ate
trac-ta-ble
treach-er-ous
tur-bu-lent
tur-pen-tine
ty-ran-nise
U-su-al
u-su-rer
u-su-ry
ut-ter-ly

Va-can-cy
vac-u-um
vag-a-bond
ve-he-ment
ven-er-ate
ven-om-ous
vet-er-an
vic-to-ry
vil-lai-ny
vi-o-late
Wick-ed-ness
wil-der-ness
won-der-ful
wor-thi-ness
wrong-ful-ly
Yel-low-ness
yes-ter-day
youth-ful-ly
Zeal-ous-ness

Words of THREE *Syllables, accented on the* SECOND.

A-ban-don
a-base-ment
a-bid-ing
a-bol-ish
a-bort-ive
ab-surd-ly
a-bun-dance
a-bus-ive
ac-cept-ance
ac-com-plish
ac-cus-tom
ac-know-ledge
ac-quaint-ance
ac-quit-tal
ad-mit-tance
ad-mon-ish
a-do-rer
a-dorn-ing

ad-van-tage
ad-ven-ture
ad-vi-ser
a-gree-ment
a-larm-ing
al-low-ance
al-migh-ty
a-maze-ment
a-mend-ment
a-muse-ment
an-gel-ic
an-noy-ance
an-oth-er
a-part-ment
ap-pel-lant
ap-pend-age
ap-point-ment
ap-pren-tice

a-quat-ic
ar-ri-val
as-sas-sin
as-sem-ble
as-sert-or
as-sess-ment
as-sum-ing
as-su-rance
as-ton-ish
a-sy-lum
ath-let-ic
a-tone-ment
at-tain-ment
at-tem-per
at-tend-ance
at-tent-ive
at-tor-ney
at-tract-ive

at-trib-ute
a-vow-al
au-then-tic
Bal-co-ny
bap-tis-mal
be-com-ing
be-fore-hand
be-gin-ning
be-hold-en
be-liev-er
be-long-ing
be-stow-er
be-tray-er
be-wil-der
bom-bard-ment
Ca-the-dral
clan-des-tine
col-lect-or
com-mand-ment
com-mit-ment
com-pen-sate
com-plete-ly
con-demn-ed
con-fis-cate
con-found-er
con-jec-ture
con-joint-ly
con-ni-vance
con-sid-er
con-sist-ent
con-sum-er
con-sump-tive
con-tem-plate
con-tent-ment
con-tin-gent
con-tri-vance
con-trol-ler
con-vert-er
con-vict-ed
cor-rect-or

cor-ro-sive
cor-rupt-ness
cre-a-tor
De-ben-ture
de-can-ter
de-ceas-ed
de-ceit-ful
de-ceiv-er
de-ci-sive
de-claim-er
de-co-rum
de-crep-id
de-fence-less
de-fen-sive
de-form-ed
de-light-ful
de-liv-er
de-lu-sive
de-mol-ish
de-mure-ness
de-ni-al
de-part-ure
de-pend-ant
de-po-nent
de-pos-it
de-scend-ant
de-sert-er
de-spond-ent
de-stroy-er
de-vour-er
dic-ta-tor
dif-fus-ive
di-min-ish
di-rect-or
dis-a-ble
dis-as-ter
dis-bur-den
dis-ci-ple
dis-cov-er
dis-cour-age

dis-dain-ful
dis-fig-ure
dis-grace-ful
dis-heart-en
dis-hon-est
dis-hon-our
dis-or-der
dis-par-age
dis-qui-et
dis-sem-ble
dis-taste-ful
dis-til-ler
dis-tinct-ly
dis-tin-guish
dis-tract-ed
dis-trib-ute
dis-trust-ful
dis-turb-ance
di-vi-ner
di-ur-nal
di-vul-ger
do-mes-tic
dra-mat-ic
Ec-lec-tic
e-clips-ed
ef-fec-tive
ef-ful-gent
e-lev-en
e-li″-cit
e-lon-gate
e-lu-sive
em-bar-go
em-bel-lish
em-broid-er
em-pan-nel
em-ploy-ment
en-a-ble
en-am-el
en-camp-ment
en-chant-er

en-count-er
en-cour-age
en-croach-ment
en-cum-ber
en-dea-vour
en-dorse-ment
en-du-rance
en-fet-ter
en-large-ment
en-light-en
en-su-rance
en-tice-ment
en-vel-op
en-vi-rons
e-pis-tle
er-ra-tic
e-stab-lish
e-ter-nal
ex-alt-ed
ex-hib-it
ex-ter-nal
ex-tin-guish
Fa-nat-ic
fan-tas-tic
fo-men-tor
for-bear-ance
for-get-ful
for-sa-ken
ful-fil-led
Gi-gan-tic
Har-mon-ics
here-af-ter
he-ro-ic
hu-mane-ly
I-de-a
il-lus-trate
im-a"-gine
im-mod-est
im-mor-tal
im-peach-ment

im-port-er
im-pos-tor
im-pris-on
im-pru-dent
in-cen-tive
in-clu-sive
in-cum-bent
in-debt-ed
in-de-cent
in-den-ture
in-duce-ment
in-dul-gence
in-for-mal
in-form-er
in-fringe-ment
in-hab-it
in-he-rent
in-he"-rit
in-hu-man
in-qui-ry
in-sip-id
in-stinct-ive
in-struct-or
in-vent-or
in-ter-nal
in-ter-pret
in-tes-tate
in-trin-sic
in-val-id
Je-ho-vah
La-con-ic
lieu-ten-ant
Ma-lig-nant
ma-raud-er
ma-ter-nal
ma-ture-ly
me-chan-ic
mi-nute-ly
mis-con-duct
mis-no-mer

mo-nas-tic
Neg-lect-ful
noc-tur-nal
Ob-ject-or
o-bli-ging
ob-lique-ly
ob-serv-ance
oc-cur-rence
of-fend-er
of-fen-sive
op-po-nent
or-gan-ic
Pa-cif-ic
par-ta-ker
pa-thet-ic
per-fu-mer
per-spec-tive
po-lite-ly
po-ma-tum
pre-pa-rer
pre-sump-tive
pro-ceed-ing
pro-duct-ive
pro-phet-ic
pro-po-sal
pros-pect-ive
Re-deem-er
re-dun-dant
re-lin-quish
re-luc-tant
re-main-der
re-mem-ber
re-mem-brance
re-miss-ness
re-morse-less
re-nown-ed
re-plen-ish
re-proach-ful
re-sem-ble
re-sis-tance

re-spect-ful	spec-ta-tor	un-god-ly
re-venge-ful	sub-mis-sive	un-grate-ful
re-view-er	Tes-ta-tor	un-ho-ly
re-vi-ler	thanks-giv-ing	un-learn-ed
re-vi-val	to-bac-co	un-ru-ly
re-volt-er	to-geth-er	un-skil-ful
re-ward-er	trans-pa-rent	un-sta-ble
Sar-cas-tic	tri-bu-nal	un-thank-ful
se-cure-ly	tri-um-phant	un-time-ly
se-duc-er	Un-cov-er	un-wor-thy
se-ques-ter	un-daunt-ed	un-com-mon.
se-rene-ly	un-e-quel	Vice-ge-rent
sin-cere-ly	un-fruit-ful	vin-dic-tive

Words of THREE *Syllables, accented on the* LAST.

Ac-qui-esce	Dis-a-buse	in-dis-creet
af-ter-noon	dis-a-gree	in-ter-cede
a-la-mode	dis-al-low	in-ter-cept
am-bus-cade	dis-ap-pear	in-ter-change
ap-per-tain	dis-ap-point	in-ter-fere
ap-pre-hend	dis-ap-prove	in-ter-lope
Bal-us-trade	dis-be-lieve	in-ter-mit
bar-ri-cade	dis-com-mend	in-ter-mix
brig-a-dier	dis-com-pose	in-ter-vene
buc-ca-neer	dis-con-tent	Mag-a-zine
Ca″-ra-van	dis-en-chant	mis-ap-ply
cav-al-cade	dis-en-gage	mis-be-have
cir-cum-scribe	dis-en-thral	O-ver-charge
cir-cum-vent	dis-o-bey	o-ver-flow
co-in-cide	En-ter-tain	o-ver-lay
com-plais-ance	Gas-con-ade	o-ver-look
com-pre-hend	gaz-et-teer	o-ver-spread
con-de-scend	Here-up-on	o-ver-take
con-tra-dict	Im-ma-ture	o-ver-throw
con-tro-vert	im-por-tune	o-ver-turn
cor-re-spond	in-com-mode	o-ver-whelm
coun-ter-mine	in-com-plete	Per-se-vere
coun-ter-vail	in-cor-rect	Re″-col-lect

re″-com-mend	re″-pri-mand	un-der-go
re-con-vene	Ser-e-nade	un-der-mine
re-in-force	su-per-scribe	un-der-stand
ref-u-gee	su-per-sede	un-der-take
rep-ar-tee	There-up-on	un-der-worth
re″-pre-hend	Un-a-ware	Vi-o-lin
re″-pre-sent	un-be-lief	vol-un-teer

Words of THREE *Syllables, pronounced as* TWO, *and accented on the* FIRST.

RULES.

Cion, sion, tion, sound like *shon,* either in the middle, or at the end of Words.
Ce, ci, sci, si, and *ti,* like *sh.*
Cial, tial, commonly sound like *shal.*

Cian, tian, like *shan.*
Cient, tient, like *shent.*
Cious, scious, and *tious,* like *shus.*
Science, tience, like *shence.*

Ac-ti-on	Man-si-on	po-ti-on
an-ci-ent	mar-ti-al	pre″-ci-ous
auc-ti-on	men-ti-on	Ques-ti-on
Cap-ti-ous	mer-si-on	quo-ti-ent
cau-ti-on	mo-ti-on	Sanc-ti-on
cau-ti-ous	Na-ti-on	sec-ti-on
con-sci-ence	no-ti-on	spe″-ci-al
con-sci-ous	nup-ti-al	spe-ci-ous
Dic-ti-on	O-ce-an	sta-ti-on
Fac-ti-on	op-ti-on	suc-ti-on
fac-ti-ous	Pac-ti-on	Ten-si-on
frac-ti-on	par-ti-al	ter-ti-an
frac-ti-ous	pas-si-on	trac-ti-on
Gra-ci-ous	pa-ti-ence	Unc-ti-on
Junc-ti-on	pa-ti-ent	Vec-ti-on
Lo-ti-on	pen-si-on	ver-si-on
lus-ci-ous	por-ti-on	vi″-si-on

Words of FOUR *Syllables, pronounced as* THREE, *and accented on the* SECOND.

(See the Rules at page 71.)

A-dop-ti-on	de-struc-ti-on	Ma-gi″-c-ian
af-fec-ti-on	de-trac-ti-on	mu-si″-ci-an
af-flic-ti-on	de-vo-ti-on	Nar-ra-ti-on
as-per-si-on	dis-cus-si-on	Ob-jec-ti-on
at-ten-ti-on	dis-sen-si-on	ob-la-ti-on
at-trac-ti-on	dis-tinc-ti-on	ob-struc-ti-on
au-spi-ci-ous	di-vi″-si-on	op-pres-si-on
Ca-pa-ci-ous	E-jec-ti-on	op-ti″-ci-an
ces-sa-ti-on	e-lec-ti-on	o-ra-ti-on
col-la-ti-on	e-rup-ti-on	Per-fec-ti-on
com-pas-si-on	es-sen-ti-al	pol-lu-ti-on
com-pul-si-on	ex-ac-ti-on	pre-dic-ti-on
con-cep-ti-on	ex-clu-si-on	pre-scrip-ti-on
con-clu-si-on	ex-pan-si-on	pro-mo-ti-on
con-fes-si-on	ex-pres-si-on	pro-por-ti-on
con-fu-si-on	ex-pul-si-on	pro-vin-ci-al
con-junc-ti-on	ex-tor-ti-on	Re-jec-ti-on
con-struc-ti-on	ex-trac-ti-on	re-la-ti-on
con-ten-ti-ous	Fal-la-ci-ous	re-ten-ti-on
con-ver-si-on	foun-da-ti-on	Sal-va-ti-on
con-vic-ti-on	Im-mer-si-on	sub-jec-ti-on
con-vul-si-on	im-par-ti-al	sub-stan-ti-al
cor-rec-ti-on	im-pa-ti-ent	sub-trac-ti-on
cor-rup-ti-on	im-pres-si-on	sub-ver-si-on
cre-a-ti-on	in-junc-ti-on	suc-ces-si-on
De-coc-ti-on	in-scrip-ti-on	suf-fi″-ci-ent
de-fec-ti-on	in-struc-ti-on	sus-pi″-ci-on
de-fi″-ci-ent	in-ven-ti-on	Temp-ta-ti-on
de-jec-ti-on	ir-rup-ti-on	trans-la-ti-on
de-li″-ci-ous	Li-cen-ti-ous	Va-ca-ti-on
de-scrip-ti-on	lo-gi″-ci-an	vex-a-ti-on

Words of FOUR *Syllables, accented on the*
FIRST.

Ab-so-lute-ly	beau-ti-ful-ly	cus-tom-a-ry
ac-ces-sa-ry	ben-e-fit-ed	cov-et-ous-ly
ac-cu-ra-cy	boun-ti-ful-ness	Dan-ger-ous-ly
ac-cu-rate-ly	bril-li-an-cy	del-i-ca-cy
a"-cri-mo-ny	bur-go-mas-ter	des-pi-ca-ble
ac-tu-al-ly	Cap-i-tal-ly	dif-fi-cul-ty
ad-di-to-ry	cas-u-ist-ry	dil-i-gent-ly
ad-e-quate-ly	cat-er-pil-lar	dis-pu-ta-ble
ad-mi-ra-ble	cel-i-ba-cy	drom-e-da-ry
ad-mi-ral-ty	cen-sur-a-ble	du-ra-ble-ness
ad-ver-sa-ry	cer-e-mo-ny	Ef-fi-ca-cy
ag-gra-va-ted	cir-cu-la-ted	el-e-gant-ly
al-a-bas-ter	cog-ni-za-ble	el-i-gi-ble
a-li-en-ate	com-fort-a-ble	em-i-nent-ly
al-le-go-ry	com-men-ta-ry	ex-cel-len-cy
al-ter-a-tive	com-mis-sa-ry	ex-e-cra-ble
a-mi-a-ble	com-mon-al-ty	ex-o-ra-ble
am-i-ca-ble	com-pa-ra-ble	ex-qui-site-ly
am-o-rous-ly	com-pe-ten-cy	Fa-vour-a-bly
an-i-ma-ted	con-fi-dent-ly	feb-ru-a-ry
an-nu-al-ly	con-quer-a-ble	fig-u-ra-tive
an-swer-a-ble	con-se-quent-ly	fluc-tu-a-ting
an-ti-cham-ber	con-sti-tu-ted	for-mi-da-ble
an-ti-mo-ny	con-ti-nent-ly	for-tu-nate-ly
an-ti-qua-ry	con-tro-ver-sy	fraud-u-lent-ly
ap-o-plec-tic	con-tu-ma-cy	friv-o-lous-ly
ap-pli-ca-ble	co-pi-ous-ly	Gen-er-al-ly
ar-bi-tra-ry	co"-py-hold-er	gen-er-ous-ly
ar-ro-gant-ly	cor-po-ral-ly	gil-li-flow-er
au-di-to-ry	cor-pu-lent-ly	gov-ern-a-ble
a-vi-a-ry	cor-ri-gi-ble	grad-a-to-ry
Bar-ba-rous-ly	cred-it-a-ble	Hab-er-dash-er

hab-it-a-ble
het-er-o-dox
hon-our-a-ble
hos-pit-a-ble
hu-mour-ous-ly
Ig-no-mi"-ny
im-i-ta-tor
in-do-lent-ly
in-no-cen-cy
in-ti-ma-cy
in-tri-ca-cy
in-ven-to-ry
Jan-u-a-ry
ju-di-ca-ture
jus-ti-fi-ed
Lap-i-da-ry
lit-er-al-ly
lit-er-a-ture
lo-gi-cal-ly
lu-mi-na-ry
Ma-gis-tra-cy
mal-le-a-ble
man-da-to-ry
ma"-tri-mo-ny
mel-an-cho-ly
mem-o-ra-ble
men-su-ra-ble
mer-ce-na-ry
mil-i-ta-ry
mis-er-a-ble
mod-er-ate-ly
mo-men-ta-ry

mon-as-te-ry
mo"-ral-i-zer
mul-ti-pli-er
mu-si-cal-ly
mu-ti-nous-ly
Na"-tu-ral-ly
ne"-ces-sa-ry
ne-cro-man-cy
neg-li-gent-ly
not-a-ble-ness
nu-mer-ous-ly
Ob-du-ra-cy
ob-sti-na-cy
ob-vi-ous-ly
oc-cu-pi-er
oc-u-lar-ly
op-er-a-tive
or-a-to-ry
or-di-na-ry
Pa"-ci-fi-er
pal-a-ta-ble
par-don-a-ble
pa"-tri-mo-ny
pen-e-tra-ble
per-ish-a-ble
prac-ti-ca-ble
preb-en-da-ry
pref-er-a-ble
pres-by-te-ry
prev-a-lent-ly
prof-it-a-ble
prom-is-so-ry

pur-ga-to-ry
pu-ri-fi-er
Rat-i-fi-er
rea-son-a-ble
righ-te-ous-ness
Sac-ri-fi-cer
sanc-tu-a-ry
sat-is-fi-ed
sec-re-ta-ry
sep-a-rate-ly
ser-vice-a-ble
slov-en-li-ness
sol-i-ta-ry
sov-er-eign-ty
spec-u-la-tive
spir-it-u-al
stat-u-a-ry
sub-lu-na-ry
Tab-er-na-cle
ter-ri-fy-ing
ter-ri-to-ry
tes-ti-mo-ny
tol-er-a-ble
tran-si-to-ry
Val-u-a-ble
va-ri-a-ble
ve"-ge-ta-ble
ven-er-a-ble
vir-tu-ous-ly
vol-un-ta-ry
War-rant-a-ble
wash-er-wo-man

Words of FOUR *Syllables, accented on the*
SECOND.

Ab-bre-vi-ate	as-tro″-no-mer	con-test-a-ble
ab-dom-i-nal	at-ten-u-ate	con-tig-u-ous
a-bil-i-ty	a-vail-a-ble	con-tin-u-al
a-bom-i-nate	au-then-ti-cate	con-trib-u-tor
a-bun-dant-ly	au-thor-i-ty	con-ve-ni-ent
a-bus-ive-ly	Bar-ba-ri-an	con-vers-a-ble
ac-cel-er-ate	be-at-i-tude	co-op-e-rate
ac-ces-si-ble	be-com-ing-ly	cor-po-re-al
ac-com-pa-ny	be-ha-vi-our	cor-rel-a-tive
ac-count-a-ble	be-ne″-fi-cence	cor-rob-o-rate
ac-cu-mu-late	be-ne″-vo-lence	cor-ro-sive-ly
a-cid-i-ty	bi-o″-gra-phy	cu-ta-ne-ous
ad-min-is-ter	bi-tu-mi-nous	De-bil-i-tate
ad-mon-ish-er	Ca-lam-i-tous	de-crep-i-tude
ad-ven-tur-er	ca-lum-ni-ous	de-fen-si-ble
a-gree-a-ble	ca-pit-u-late	de-fin-i-tive
al-low-a-ble	ca-tas-tro-phe	de-form-i-ty
am-bas-sa-dor	cen-so-ri-ous	de-gen-er-ate
am-big-u-ous	chi-rur-gi-cal	de-ject-ed-ly
am-phi″-bi-ous	chro-no″-lo-gy	de-lib-er-ate
a-na″-to-mist	con-form-a-ble	de-light-ful-ly
an-gel-i-cal	con-grat-u-late	de-lin-e-ate
an-ni-hil-ate	con-sid-er-ate	de-liv-er-ance
a-nom-a-lous	con-sist-o-ry	de-mo″-cra-cy
an-tag-o-nist	con-sol-i-date	de-mon-stra-ble
an-ti″-pa-thy	con-spic-u-ous	de-nom-i-nate
an-ti″-qui-ty	con-spi″-ra-cy	de-plo-ra-ble
a-po″-lo-gize	con-su-ma-ble	de-pop-u-late
a-rith-me-tic	con-sist-en-cy	de-pre-ci-ate
as-sas-sin-ate	con-tam-i-nate	de-si-ra-ble
as-tro″-lo-ger	con-tempt-i-ble	de-spite-ful-ly

de-spond-en-cy
de-ter-min-ate
de-test-a-ble
dex-te″-ri-ty
di-min-u-tive
dis-cern-i-ble
dis-cov-e-ry
dis-crim-i-nate
dis-dain-ful-ly
dis-grace-ful-ly
dis-loy-al-ty
dis-or-der-ly
dis-pen-sa-ry
dis-sat-is-fy
dis-sim-i-lar
dis-u-ni-on
div-in-i-ty
dog-mat-i-cal
dox-o″-lo-gy
du-pli″-ci-ty
E-bri-e-ty
ef-fec-tu-al
ef-fem-i-nate
ef-fron-te-ry
e-gre-gi-ous
e-jac-u-late
e-lab-o-rate
e-lu-ci-date
e-mas-cu-late
em-pir-i-cal
em-pov-er-ish
en-am-el-ler
en-thu-si-ast
e-nu-mer-ate

e-pis-co-pal
e-pit-o-me
e-quiv-o-cate
er-ro-ne-ous
e-the-re-al
e-van-gel-ist
e-vap-o-rate
e-va-sive-ly
e-ven-tu-al
ex-am-in-er
ex-ceed-ing-ly
ex-ces-sive-ly
ex-cu-sa-ble
ex-ec-u-tor
ex-em-pla-ry
ex-fo-li-ate
ex-hil-a-rate
ex-on-er-ate
ex-or-bi-tant
ex-pe″-ri-ment
ex-ter-mi-nate
ex-trav-a-gant
ex-trem-i-ty
Fa-nat-i-cism
fas-tid-i-ous
fa-tal-i-ty
fe-li″-ci-ty
fra-gil-i-ty
fru-gal-i-ty
fu-tu-ri-ty
Ge-o″-gra-phy
ge-o″-me-try
gram-ma-ri-an
gram-mat-i-cal

Ha-bil-i-ment
ha-bit-u-ate
har-mon-i-cal
her-met-i-cal
hi-la″-ri-ty
hu-man-i-ty
hu-mil-i-ty
hy-po″-the-sis
I-dol-a-ter
il-lit-er-ate
il-lus-tri-ous
im-men-si-ty
im-mor-tal-ize
im-mu-ta-ble
im-ped-i-ment
im-pen-i-tence
im-pe-ri-ous
im-per-ti-nent
im-pet-u-ous
im-pi-e-ty
im-plac-a-ble
im-pol-i-tic
im-por-tu-nate
im-pos-si-ble
im-prob-a-ble
im-pov-er-ish
im-preg-na-ble
im-prov-a-ble
im-prov-i-dent
in-an-i-mate
in-au-gu-rate
in-ca-pa-ble
in-clem-en-cy
in-cli-na-ble

in-con-stan-cy
in-cu-ra-ble
in-de-cen-cy
in-el-e-gant
in-fat-u-ate
in-hab-i-tant
in-grat-i-tude
in-sin-u-ate
in-teg-ri-ty
in-ter-pre-ter
in-tract-a-ble
in-trep-id-ly
in-val-i-date
in-vet-er-ate
in-vid-i-ous
ir-rad-i-ate
i-tin-er-ant
Ju-rid-i-cal
La-bo-ri-ous
le-git-i-mate
le-gu-mi-nous
lux-u-ri-ous
Mag-ni″-ficent
ma-te-ri-al
me-tro″-po-lis
mi-rac-u-lous
Na-tiv-i-ty
non-sen-si-cal
no-to-ri-ous

O-be-di-ent
ob-serv-a-ble
om-ni″-po-tent
o-rac-u-lar
o-ri″-gi-nal
Par-tic-u-lar
pe-nu-ri-ous
per-pet-u-al
per-spic-u-ous
phi-lo″-so-pher
pos-te-ri-or
pre-ca-ri-ous
pre-cip-i-tate
pre-des-ti-nate
pre-dom-i-nate
pre-oc-cu-py
pre-va″-ri-cate
pro-gen-i-tor
pros-per-i-ty
Ra-pid-i-ty
re-cep-ta-cle
re-cum-ben-cy
re-cur-ren-cy
re-deem-a-ble
re-dun-dan-cy
re-frac-to-ry
re-gen-er-ate
re-luc-tan-cy
re-mark-a-ble

re-mu-ner-ate
re-splen-dent-ly
re-sto-ra-tive
re-su-ma-ble
Sa-ga″-ci-ty
si-mil-i-tude
sim-pli″-ci-ty
so-lem-ni-ty
so-li″-ci-tor
so-li″-ci-tous
sub-ser-vi-ent
su-pe-ri-or
su-per-la-tive
su-prem-a-cy
Tau-to″-lo-gy
ter-ra-que-ous
ther-mo″-me-ter
the-o″-lo-gy
tri-um-phant-ly
tu-mul-tu-ous
ty-ran-ni-cal
U-nan-i-mous
u-bi″-qui-ty
un-search-a-ble
Va-cu-i-ty
ver-nac-u-lar
vi-cis-si-tude
vi-va″-ci-ty
vo-lup-tu-ous

SELECT FABLES.

THE FARTHING RUSHLIGHT.

Once a Rushlight, in love with its own brilliancy, boasted that its light was brighter than that of the sun, the moon, and the stars. Just then it was blown out by the wind. A girl who relit it, said, "Cease your boasting; Heavenly lights do not blow out."

THE BOY AND THE NETTLES.

A Boy was stung by a Nettle. He ran home and told his mother, saying, "Although it pains me so much, I did but touch it ever so gently." "That was just it," said his mother, "which caused it to sting you. The next time you touch a Nettle, grasp it boldly, and it will be soft as silk to your hand, and not in the least hurt you."

Whatever you do, do with all your might.

THE MOTHER AND THE WOLF.

A famished Wolf was prowling about in the morning in search of food. As he passed the door of a cottage built in the forest, he heard a Mother say to her child, " Be quiet, or I will throw you out of the window, and the Wolf shall eat you." The Wolf sat all day waiting at the door. In the evening he heard the same woman, fondling her child and saying: "He is quiet now, and if the Wolf should come, we will kill him." The Wolf, hearing these words, went home, gaping with cold and hunger. On his reaching his den, Mistress Wolf inquired of him why he returned wearied and supperless, so contrary to his wont. He replied: "Why, forsooth! —because I gave credence to the words of a woman!"

KG.

THE DOG AND THE SHADOW.

A Dog, crossing a bridge over a stream with a piece of flesh in his mouth, saw his own shadow in the water, and took it for that of another Dog, with a piece of meat double his own in size. He therefore let go his own, and fiercely attacked

the other Dog, to get his larger piece from him.
He thus lost both : that which he grasped at in
the water, because it was a shadow ; and his
own, because the stream swept it away.

THE WOMAN AND HER HEN.

A Woman possessed a Hen that gave her an
egg every day. She often thought with herself
how she might obtain two eggs daily instead of
one, and at last, to gain her purpose, determined
to give the Hen a double allowance of barley.
From that day the Hen became fat and sleek,
and never once laid another egg.

Covetousness overreacheth itself.

THE MILK-WOMAN AND HER PAIL.

A Farmer's daughter was carrying her pail of milk from the field to the farm-house, when she fell a-musing. "The money for which this milk will be sold, will buy at least three hundred eggs. The eggs, allowing for all mishaps, will produce two hundred and fifty chickens. The chickens will become ready for the market when poultry will fetch the highest price; so that by the end of the year I shall have money enough from the perquisites that will fall to my share, to buy a new gown. In this dress I will go to the Christmas junketings, when all the young fellows will propose to me, but I will toss my head, and refuse them every one." At this moment she tossed her head in unison with her thoughts, when down fell the Milk-pail to the ground, and all her imaginary schemes perished in a moment.

THE HARE AND THE TORTOISE.

A Hare one day ridiculed the short feet and slow pace of the Tortoise. The latter, laughing, said, "Though you be swift as the wind, I will beat you in a race." The Hare, deeming her assertion to be simply impossible, assented to the proposal; and they agreed that the Fox should choose the course, and fix the goal. On the day appointed for the race they started together. The Tortoise never for a moment stopped, but went on with a slow but steady pace straight to the end of the course. The Hare, trusting to his native swiftness, cared little about the race, and lying down by the wayside, fell fast asleep. At last waking up, and moving as fast as he could, he saw the Tortoise had reached the goal, and was comfortably dozing after her fatigue.

INDUSTRY AND INDOLENCE.

CONTRASTED.

A Tale by Dr. Percival.

IN a village, at a small distance from the metropolis, lived a wealthy husbandman, who had two sons, William and Thomas; the former of whom was exactly a year older than the other.

On the day when the second son was born, the husbandman planted in his orchard two young apple-trees of an equal size, on which he bestowed the same care in cultivating; and they throve so much alike, that it was a difficult matter to say which claimed the preference.

As soon as the children were capable of using garden implements, their father took them, on a fine day, early in the spring, to see the two plants he had reared for them, and called after their names. William and Thomas having much admired the beauty of these trees, now filled with blossoms, their father told them, that he made them a present of the trees in good condition, which would continue to thrive or decay, in proportion to the labour or neglect they received.

Thomas, though the youngest son, turned all his attention to the improvement of his tree, by clearing it of insects as soon as he discovered them, and propping up the stem that it might grow perfectly upright. He dug about it, to loosen the earth, that the root might receive nourishment from the warmth of the sun, and the moisture of the dews. No mother could nurse her child more tenderly in its infancy, than Thomas did his tree.

His brother William, however, pursued a very different conduct; for he loitered away all his time in the most idle and mischievous manner, one of his principal amusements being to throw stones at people as they passed. He kept company with all the idle boys in the neighbourhood, with whom he was continually fighting, and was seldom without either a black eye or a broken skin. His poor tree was neglected, and never thought of, till one day in autumn, when, by chance, seeing his brother's tree loaded with the finest apples, and almost ready to break down with the weight, he ran to his own tree, not doubting that he should find it in the same pleasing condition.

Great, indeed, were his disappointment and surprise, when, instead of finding the tree loaded with excellent fruit, he beheld nothing but a few withered leaves, and branches covered with moss. He instantly went to his father, and complained of his partiality in giving him a tree that was worthless and barren, while his brother's produced the most luxuriant fruit; and he thought that his brother should, at least, give him half of his apples.

His father told him that it was by no means reasonable that the industrious should give up part of their labour to feed the idle. " If your tree," said he, " has produced you nothing, it is but a just reward of your indolence, since you see what the industry of your brother has gained him. Your tree was equally full of blossoms, and grew in the same soil ; but you paid no attention to the culture of it. Your brother suffered no visible insects to remain on his tree ; but you neglected that caution, and suffered them to eat up the very buds. As I cannot bear to see even plants perish through neglect, I must now take this tree from you, and give it to your brother, whose care and attention may possibly restore it to its former vigour. The fruit it produces shall be his property, and you must no longer consider yourself as having any right in it. However, you may go to my nursery, and there choose any other you may like better, and try what you can do with it ; but if you neglect to take proper care of it, I shall take that also from you, and give it to your brother as a reward for his superior industry and attention."

This had the desired effect on William, who clearly perceived the justice and propriety of his father's reasoning, and instantly went into the nursery to choose the most thriving apple-tree he could meet with. His brother Thomas, assisting him in the culture of his tree, advised him in what manner to proceed ; and William made the best use of his time, and the instructions he received from his brother. He left off all his mischievous tricks, forsook the company of idle boys, applied himself cheerfully to work, and in autumn received the reward of his labour, his tree being loaded with fruit.

MORAL *and* PRACTICAL OBSERVATIONS, *which ought
to be committed to memory at an early age.*

It is wiser to prevent a quarrel, than to revenge it.

Custom is the plague of wise men : but is the idol
of fools.

He is always rich, who considers himself as having
enough.

The golden rule of happiness is to be moderate in
your expectations.

Prosperity gains friends, and adversity tries them.

Diligence, industry, and submission to advice, are
material duties of the young.

It is better to reprove, than to be angry secretly.

Anger may glance into the breast of a wise man,
but it rests only in the bosom of fools.

Sincerity and truth are the foundations of all
virtue.

By others' faults, wise men correct their own.

To mourn without measure, is folly; not to
mourn at all, is insensibility.

Industry is the parent of every excellence.

Beware of false reasoning, when you are about to inflict an injury which you cannot repair.

He can never have a true friend, who is often changing his friendships.

Virtuous youth gradually produces flourishing manhood.

None more impatiently suffer injuries, than those that are most forward in doing them.

Money, like manure, does no good till it is spread.

There is no real use in riches, except in the distribution of them.

Complaisance renders a superior amiable, an equal agreeable, and an inferior acceptable.

Excess of ceremony shews want of breeding.

By taking revenge of an injury, a man is only even with his enemy; by passing it over, he is superior.

No object is more pleasing to the eye, than the sight of a man whom you have obliged.

No music is so agreeable to the ear, as the voice of one that owns you for his benefactor.

The only benefit to be derived from flattery is, that by hearing what we are not, we may be instructed in what we ought to be.

A wise man will desire no more than what he may get justly, use soberly, distribute cheerfully, and live upon contentedly.

The character of the person who commends you, is to be considered, before you set much value on his praise.

Ingratitude is a crime so shameful, that no man was ever found, who would acknowledge himself guilty of it.

A wise man applauds him whom he thinks most virtuous; the rest of the world, him who is most powerful, or most wealthy.

There is more trouble in accumulating the first hundred, than in the next five thousand.

Fix on that course of life which is the most excellent, and habit will render it the most delightful.

As to be perfectly just is an attribute of the divine nature, to be so to the utmost of his abilities, is the glory of man.

No man was ever cast down with the injuries of fortune, unless he had before suffered himself to be deceived by her favours.

Nothing engages more the affections of men, then a polite address, and graceful conversation.

A more glorious victory cannot be gained over another man, than to return injury with kindness.

There cannot be a greater treachery, than first to raise confidence, and then deceive it.

It is as great a point of wisdom to hide ignorance, as to discover knowledge.

No man hath a thorough taste of prosperity, to whom adversity never happened.

There is a tide in the affairs of men, which taken at the flood leads on to fortune.

Beware of making a false estimate of your own powers, character, and pretensions.

The man who tells nothing, or who tells everything, will equally have nothing told him.

A lie is always troublesome, sets a man's invention upon the rack, and requires the aid of many more to support it.

We should take prudent care for the future; but not so as to spoil the enjoyment of the present.

It forms no part of wisdom to be miserable to-day, because we may happen to become so to-morrow.

It is the infirmity of little minds, to be captivated by every appearance, and dazzled with every thing that sparkles.

The heart of fools is in their mouth, but the tongue of the wise is in his heart.

He that is truly polite, knows how to contradict with respect, and to please without adulation.

A good word is an easy obligation, but not to speak ill, requires only our silence, and costs us nothing.

The manners of a well-bred man are equally remote from insipid complaisance, and low familiarity.

Wisdom is the grey hairs to a man, and an unspotted life is the most venerable old age.

Let reason go before every enterprise. and counsel before every action.

Most men are friends for their own purposes, and will not abide in the day of trouble.

A friend cannot be known in prosperity; and an enemy cannot be hidden in adversity.

He who discovereth secrets, loseth his credit, and will never secure valuable friendships.

Honour thy father with thy whole heart, and forget not the kindness of thy mother; how canst thou recompense them the things they have done for thee?

He who tells a lie, is not sensible how great a task he undertakes; for he is forced to invent many more to maintain it.

The prodigal robs his heir, the miser robs himself.

True wisdom consists in the regulation and government of the passions; and not in a technical knowledge of arts and sciences.

Economy is no disgrace; it is better to live on a little, than to outlive a great deal.

Almost all difficulties are to be overcome by industry and perseverance.

A small injury done to another, is a great injury done to yourself.

He that sows thistles will not reap wheat.

The weapon of the wise is reason; the weapon of fools is steel.

Never defer that till to-morrow, which can be as well performed to-day.

You must convince men before you can reform them.

Habits of tenderness towards the meanest animals, beget habits of charity and benevolence towards our fellow-creatures.

A man's fortunes may always be retrieved, if he has retained habits of sobriety and industry.

ADVICE TO YOUNG PERSONS INTENDED FOR TRADE.

By Dr. Benjamin Franklin.

REMEMBER *that time is money.*—He that can earn ten shillings a-day at his labour, and goes abroad, or sits idle one half of that day, though he spends but sixpence during his diversion or idleness, ought not to reckon *that* the only expense ; he has spent, or rather thrown away, five shillings besides.

Remember that credit is money.—If a man lets his money lie in my hands after it is due, because he has a good opinion of my credit, he gives me the interest, or so much as I can make of the money during that time. This amounts to a considerable sum where a man has large credit, and makes good use of it.

Remember that money is of a prolific or multiplying nature.—Money can produce money, and its offspring can produce more and so on. Five shillings turned is six ; turned again, it is seven and three-pence ; and so on, till it becomes a hundred pounds. The more there is of it, the more it produces every turning, so that the profits rise quicker and quicker. He that throws away a crown, destroys all that it might have produced, even scores of pounds.

Remember that six pounds a year is but a groat a day.— For this little sum (which may be daily wasted, either in time or expense, unperceived) a man of credit may, on his own security, have the constant possession and use of a hundred pounds. So much in stock, briskly turned by an industrious man, produces great advantage.

Remember this saying, " *The good paymaster is lord of another man's purse.*"—He that is known to pay punctually and exactly to the time he promises. may at any time, and on any occasion, raise all the money his friends can spare. This is sometimes of great use. Next to industry and frugality, nothing contributes more to the raising of a man in the world, than punctuality and justice in all·his dealings ; therefore never keep borrowed money an hour beyond the time promised, lest a disappointment shut up your friend's purse for ever.

The most trifling actions that affect a man's credit are to be regarded.—The sound of the hammer at five in the morning, or nine at night, heard by a creditor, makes him easy six months longer; but if he sees you at a billiard-table, or hears your voice at a tavern, when you should be at work, he sends for his money the next day, and demands it before it is convenient for you to pay him.

In short, the way to wealth, if you desire it, is as plain as the way to market. It depends chiefly on two things, *industry* and *frugality;* that is, waste neither *time* nor *money,* but make the best use of both.

GOLDEN RULES FOR YOUNG SHOPKEEPERS.
By Sir Richard Phillips.

1. Choose a good and commanding situation, even at a higher rate or premium; for no money is so well laid out as for situation, providing good use be made of it.

2. Take your shop door off the hinges at seven o'clock every morning, that no obstruction may be opposed to your customers.

3. Clean and set out your windows before seven o'clock, and do this with your own hands, that you may expose for sale the articles which are most saleable, and which you most want to sell.

4. Sweep before your house; and, if required, open a footway from the opposite side of the street, that passengers may think of you while crossing, and that all your neighbours may be sensible of your diligence.

5. Wear an apron, if such be the custom of your business, and consider it as a badge of distinction, which will procure you respect and credit.

6. Apply your first return of ready money to pay debts before they are due, and give such transactions suitable emphasis by claiming discount.

7. Always be found at home, and in some way employed; and remember that your meddling neighbours have their eyes upon you, and are constantly gauging you by your appearances.

8. Re-weigh and re-measure all your stock, rather than let it be supposed you have nothing to do.

9. Keep some article cheap, that you may draw customers and enlarge your intercourse.

10. Keep up the exact quality, or flavour, of all articles which you find are approved of by your customers; and by this means you will enjoy their preference.

11. Buy for ready money as often as you have any to spare; and when you take credit, pay to a day, and unasked.

12. No advantage will ever arise to you, from any ostentatious display of expenditure.

13. Beware of the odds and ends of a stock, of remnants, of spoiled goods, and of waste, for it is in such things that your profits lie.

14. In serving your customers be firm and obliging, and never lose your temper,—for nothing is got by it.

15. Always be seen at church or chapel on Sunday; never at a gaming table: and seldom at theatres or at places of amusement.

16. Prefer a prudent and discreet, to a rich and showy wife.

17. Spend your evenings by your own fire-side, and shun a public-house or a sottish club, as you would a bad debt.

18. Subscribe with your neighbours to a book-club, and improve your mind, that you may be qualified to use your future affluence with credit to yourself, and advantage to the public.

19. Take stock every year, estimate your profits, and do not spend above one fourth.

20. Avoid the common folly of expending your precious capital upon a costly architectural front; such things operate on the world like paint on a woman's cheek,—repelling beholders instead of attracting them.

21. Every pound wasted by a young tradesman is two pounds lost at the end of three years, and two hundred and fifty-six pounds at the end of twenty-four years.

22. To avoid being robbed and ruined by apprentices and assistants, never allow them to go from home in the evening; and the restriction will prove equally useful to master and servant.

23. Remember that prudent purchasers avoid the shop of an extravagant and ostentatious trader; for they justly consider, that, if they deal with him, they must contribute to his follies.

24. Let these be your rules till you have realised your stock, and till you can take discount for prompt payment on all purchases; and you may then indulge in any degree which your habits and sense of prudence suggest.

Alphabetical Collection of *Words, nearly the same in Sound, but different in Spelling and Signification.*

Accidence, a book
Accidents, chances
Account, esteem
Accompt, reckoning
Acts, deeds
Ax, a hatchet
Hacks, doth hack
Adds, doth add
Adze, a cooper's axe
Ail, to be ill
Ale, malt liquor
Hail, to salute
Hail, frozen rain
Hale, strong
Air, to breathe
Heir, oldest son
Hair, of the head
Hare, an animal
Are, they be
Ere, before
All, every one
Awl, to bore with
Hall, a large room
Haul, to pull
Allowed, granted
Aloud, with a noise
Altar, for sacrifice
Alter, to change
Halter, a rope
Ant, an emmet
Aunt, parent's sister
Haunt, to frequent
Ascent, going up
Assent, agreement
Assistance, help
Assistants, helpers
Augur, a soothsayer
Auger, a carpenter's tool

Bail, a surety
Bale, a large parcel
Ball, a sphere
Bawl, to cry out
Beau, a fop
Bow, to shoot with
Bear, to carry
Bear, a beast
Bare, naked
Base, mean
Bass, a part in music
Base, bottom
Bays, bay leaves
Be, the verb
Bee, an insect
Beer, a drink
Bier, a carriage for the dead
Bean, a kind of pulse
Been, from to *be*
Beat, to strike
Beet, a root
Bell, to ring
Belle, a young lady
Berry, a small fruit
Bury, to inter
Blew, did blow
Blue, a colour
Boar, a beast
Boor, a clown
Bore, to make a hole
Bore, did bear
Bolt, a fastening
Boult, to sift meal
Boy, a lad
Buoy, a water mark
Bread, baked flour
Bred, brought up
Burrow, a hole in the earth

Borough, a corporation
By, near
Buy, to purchase
Bye, indirectly
Brews, breweth
Bruise, to crush
But, except
Butt, two hogsheads
Calendar, almanack
Calender, to smooth
Cannon, a great gun
Canon, a law
Canvas, coarse cloth
Canvass, to examine
Cart, a carriage
Chart, a map
Cell, a cave
Sell, to dispose of '
Cellar, under ground
Seller, one who sells
Censer, for incense
Censor, a critic
Censure, blame
Cession, resigning
Session, assize
Centaury, an herb
Century, 100 years
Sentry, a guard
Choler, anger
Collar, for the neck
Ceiling, of a room
Sealing, of a letter
Clause, of a sentence
Claws, of a bird or beast
Coarse, not fine
Course, a race

Corse, a dead body

Complement, full number

Compliment, to speak politely

Concert, of music

Consort, a companion

Cousin, a relation

Cozen, to cheat

Council, an assembly

Counsel, advice

Cruise, to sail up and down

Crews, ships' companies

Currant, a small fruit

Current, a stream

Creek, of the sea

Creak, to make a noise

Cygnet, a young swan

Signet, a seal

Dear, of great value

Deer, in a park

Dew, moisture

Due, owing

Descent, going down

Dissent, to disagree

Dependance, trust

Dependants, those who are subject

Devices, inventions

Devises, contrives

Decease, death

Disease, disorder

Doe, a she-deer

Dough, paste

Done, performed

Dun, a colour

Dun, a troublesome creditor

Draught, of drink

Draft, drawing

Urn, a vessel

Earn, to gain by labour

East, a point of the compass

Yeast, barm

Eminent, noted

Imminent, impending

Ewe, a female sheep

Yew, a tree

You, thou or ye

Hew, to cut

Hue, colour

Hugh, a man's name

Your, a pronoun

Ewer, a kind of jug

Eye, to see with

I, myself

Fain, gladly

Fane, a temple

Feign, to dissemble

Faint, weary

Feint, pretence

Fair, handsome

Fair, merry-making

Fare, charge

Fare, food

Feet, part of the body

Feat, exploit

File, a steel instrument

Foil, to overcome

Fillip, a snap with the finger

Philip, a man's name

Fir, a tree

Fur, of a skin

Flee, to run away

Flea, an insect

Flew, did fly

Flue, down

Flue, of a chimney

Flour, ground wheat

Flower, of the field

Forth, abroad

Fourth, the number

Frays, quarrels

Phrase, a sentence

Frances, a woman's name

Francis, a man's name

Gesture, action

Jester, a joker

Gilt, with gold

Guilt, sin

Grate, a fireplace

Great, large

Grater, for nutmeg

Greater, larger

Groan, a sigh

Grown, increased

Guess, to think

Guest, a visitor

Hart, a deer

Heart, in the cavity of the chest

Art, skill

Heal, to cure

Heel, part of the foot

Eel, a fish

Helm, a rudder

Elm, a tree

Hear, the sense

Here, in this place

Heard, did hear

Herd, cattle

I, myself

Hie, to haste

High, lofty

Hire, wages
Ire, great anger
Him, from *he*
Hymn, a song
Hole, a cavity
Whole, not broken
Hoop, for a tub
Whoop, to halloo
Host, a great number
Host, a landlord
Idle, lazy
Idol, an image
Aisle, of a church
Isle, an island
Impostor, a cheat
Imposture, deceit
In, within
Inn, a public house
Incite, to stir up
Insight, knowledge
Indite, to dictate
Indict, to accuse
Ingenious, skilful
Ingenuous, frank
Intense, excessive
Intents, purposes
Kill, to murder
Kiln, to dry malt on
Knave, a rogue
Nave, middle of a wheel
Knead, to work dough
Need, want
Knew, did know
New, not worn
Knight, a title of honour
Night, darkness
Key, for a lock
Quay, a wharf
Knot, to tie
Not, denying

Know, to understand
No, not
Leak, to run out
Leek, a kind of onion
Lease, a letting
Lees, dregs
Leash, three
Lead, a metal
Led, conducted
Least, smallest
Lest, for fear
Lessen, to make less
Lesson, in reading
Lo, behold
Low, mean, humble
Loose, slack
Lose, not win
Lore, learning
Lower, more low
Made, finished
Maid, a virgin
Main, chief
Mane, of a horse
Male, he
Mail, armour
Mail, post-coach
Manner, custom
Manor, a lordship
Mare, a she-horse
Mayor, of a town
Marshal, a general
Martial, warlike
Mean, low
Mean, to intend
Mean, middle
Mien, air, look
Meat, flesh
Meet, fit
Mete, to measure
Meddler, a busybody

Medlar, a fruit
Message, an errand
Messuage, a house
Metal, substance
Mettle, vigour
Might, power
Mite, an insect
Moan, lamentation
Mown, cut down
Moat, a ditch
Mote, spot in the eye
Moor, a fen or marsh
More, in quantity
Mortar, to pound in
Mortar, made of lime
Muslin, fine linen
Muzzling, tying the mouth
Naught, bad
Nought, nothing
Nay, denying
Neigh, as a horse
Noose, a knot
News, tidings
Oar, to row with
Ore, uncast metal
Of, belonging to
Off, at a distance
Oh, alas !
Owe, to be indebted
Old, aged
Hold, to keep
One, in number
Won, did win
Our, of us
Hour, sixty minutes
Pail, a bucket
Pale, colour
Pale, a fence
Pain, torment

Pane, a square of glass
Pair, two
Pare, to peel
Pear, a fruit
Palate, of the mouth
Pallet, a painter's board
Pallet, a little bed
Pastor, a minister
Pasture, grazing land
Patience, mildness
Patients, sick people
Peace, quietness
Piece, a part
Peer, a nobleman
Pier, of a bridge
Pillar, a column
Pillow, to lay the head on
Pint, half a quart
Point, a sharp end
Place, situation
Plaice, a fish
Pray, to beseech
Prey, booty
Precedent, an example
President, governor
Principal, chief
Principle, rule or cause
Raise, to lift
Rays, beams of light
Raisin, a dried grape
Reason, argument
Relic, remainder
Relict, a widow
Right, just, true

Right, one hand
Rite, a ceremony
Sail, of a ship
Sale, the act of selling
Salary, wages
Celery, an herb
Scent, a smell
Sent, ordered away
Sea, the ocean
See, to view
Seam, a joining
Seem, to pretend
So, thus
Sow, to cast seed
Sew, with a needle
Sole, alone
Sole, of the foot
Soul, the spirit
Soar, to mount
Sore, a wound
Some, part
Sum, amount
Straight, direct
Strait, narrow
Sweet, not sour
Suite, attendants
Surplice, white robe
Surplus, over and above
Subtile, fine, thin
Subtle, cunning
Talents, good parts
Talons, claws
Team, of horses
Teem, to overflow
Tenor, intent
Tenure, occupation
Their, belonging to them
There, in that place

Threw, did throw
Through, all along
Thyme, an herb
Time, duration
Treaties, conventions
Treatise, a discourse
Vain, foolish
Vane, a weathercock
Vein, a blood-vessel
Vial, a small bottle
Viol, a fiddle
Wain, a cart or waggon
Wane, to decrease
Wait, to stay
Weight, for scales
Wet, moist
Whet, to sharpen
Wail, to mourn
Whale, a fish
Ware, merchandise
Wear, to put on
Were, from *to be*
Where, in what place
Way, road
Weigh, in scales
Wey, a measure
Whey, of milk
Week, seven days
Weak, faint
Weather, state of the air
Whether, if
Wither, to decay
Whither, to which place
Which, what
Witch, a sorceress

SELECT PIECES OF POETRY.

OMNIPOTENCE.

THE spacious firmament on high,
With all the blue ethereal sky,
And spangled heavens, a shining frame,
Their great original proclaim :
Th' unwearied sun, from day to day,
Does his Creator's power display,
And publishes to every land
The work of an Almighty hand.

Soon as the evening shades prevail,
The moon takes up the wond'rous tale
And, nightly, to the list'ning earth,
Repeats the story of her birth :

While all the stars that round her burn,
And all the planets, in their turn,
Confess the tidings as they roll,
And spread the truth from pole to pole.

What though in solemn silence all
Move round this dark terrestrial ball
What though no real voice nor sound
Amid the radiant orbs be found ;
In reason's ear they all rejoice,
And utter forth a glorious voice,
For ever singing, as they shine,
"The Hand that made us is divine.

THE BIBLE THE BEST OF BOOKS.

WHAT taught me that a Great First Cause
Existed ere creation was,
And gave a universe its laws?   The Bible.

What guide can lead me to this power,
Whom conscience calls me to adore,
And bids me seek him more and more ?   The Bible.

When all my actions prosper well,
And higher hopes my wishes swell,
What points where truer blessings dwell ?   The Bible.

When passions with temptations join,
To conquer every power of mine,
What leads me then to help divine ?   The Bible.

When pining cares, and wasting pain,
My spirits and my life-blood drain,
What soothes and turns e'en these to gain?   The Bible.

When crosses and vexations teaze,
And various ills my bosom seize,
What is it that in life can please?   The Bible.

When horror chills my soul with fear,
And nought but gloom and dread appear,
What is it then my mind can cheer?   The Bible.

When impious doubts my thoughts perplex,
And mysteries my reason vex,
Where is the guide which then directs?   The Bible.

And when affliction's fainting breath,
Warns me I've done with all beneath,
What can compose my soul in death?   The Bible.

DUTY TO GOD AND OUR NEIGHBOURS.

LOVE God with all your soul and strength
    With all your heart and mind;
And love your neighbour as yourself—
    Be faithful, just, and kind.

Deal with another as you'd have
    Another deal with you;
What you're unwilling to receive,
    Be sure you never do.

THE BLIND BOY.

O SAY, what is that thing call'd light,
  Which I must ne'er enjoy?
What are the blessings of the sight?
  O tell your poor Blind Boy!

You talk of won'drous things you see;
  You say the sun shines bright;
I feel him warm, but how can he
  Or make it day or night?

My day and night myself I make,
  Whene'er I sleep or play;
And could I always keep awake,
  With me 'twere always day.

With heavy sighs I often hear
  You mourn my hapless woe;
But sure with patience I can bear
  A loss I ne'er can know.

Then let not what I cannot have
  My cheer of mind destroy,
While thus I sing, I am a king,
  Although a poor Blind Boy.

THE TWENTY-THIRD PSALM.

THE Lord my pasture shall prepare,
And feed me with a shepherd's care;
His presence shall my wants supply,
And guard me with a watchful eye;
My noon-day walks he shall attend,
And all my midnight hours defend.

When in the sultry glebe I faint,
Or on the thirsty mountain pant;
To fertile vales, and dewy meads,
My weary wandering steps he leads;
Where peaceful rivers, soft and slow,
Amidst the verdant landscape flow.

Though in the path of death I tread,
With gloomy horrors overspread
My steadfast heart shall fear no ill;
For thou, O Lord! art with me still.
Thy friendly crook shall give me aid,
And guide me through the dreadful shade.

Though in a bare and rugged way,
Through devious lonely wilds I stray,
Thy bounty shall my pains beguile:
The barren wilderness shall smile,
With sudden green and herbage crown'd,
And streams shall murmur all around.

CRUELTY TO ANIMALS.

I WOULD not enter on my list of friends
(Though grac'd with polish'd manners and fine sense,
Yet wanting sensibility) the man
Who needlessly sets foot upon a worm.
An inadvertent step may crush the snail
That crawls at ev'ning in the public path;
But he that has humanity, forwarn'd,
Will tread aside and let the reptile live.
For they are all, the meanest things that are,
As free to live and to enjoy that life,
As God was free to form them at the first,
Who in his sov'reign wisdom made them all.

THE BEGGAR'S PETITION.

PITY the sorrows of a poor old man,
    Whose trembling steps have borne him to your door,
Whose days are dwindled to the shortest span,
    Oh! give relief, and Heav'n will bless your store.

These tatter'd clothes my poverty bespeak,
    These hoary locks proclaim my lengthen'd years,
And many a furrow in my grief-worn cheek,
    Has been a channel to a flood of tears.

Yon house erected on the rising ground,
　　With tempting aspect drew me from the road;
For Plenty there a residence has found,
　　And Grandeur a magnificent abode.

Hard is the fate of the infirm and poor!
　　Here, as I crav'd a morsel of their bread,
A pamper'd menial drove me from the door,
　　To seek a shelter in an humbler shed.

Oh! take me to your hospitable dome;
　　Keen blows the wind, and piercing is the cold;
Short is my passage to the friendly tomb;
　　For I am poor, and miserably old.

Pity the sorrows of a poor old man,
　　Whose trembling steps have borne him to your door,
Whose days are dwindled to the shortest span,
　　Oh! give relief, and Heav'n will bless your store.

MY MOTHER.

WHO fed me from her gentle breast,
And hush'd me in her arms to rest,
And on my cheek sweet kisses prest?　　My Mother.

When sleep forsook my open eye,
Who was it sung sweet lullaby,
And sooth'd me that I should not cry?　　My Mother.

Who sat and watch'd my infant head,
When sleeping on my cradle bed;
And tears of sweet affection shed?　　My Mother.

When pain and sickness made me cry,
Who gaz'd upon my heavy eye,
And wept, for fear that I should die?　　My Mother.

Who lov'd to see me pleased and gay,
And taught me sweetly how to play,
And minded all I had to say?　　My Mother.

Who ran to help me when I fell,
And would some pretty story tell,
Or kiss the place to make it well?　　My Mother.

Who taught my infant heart to pray,
And love God's holy book and day;
And taught me Wisdom's pleasant way?　　My Mother.

And can I ever cease to be
Affectionate and kind to thee,
Who wast so very kind to me,   My Mother.

Ah, no ! the thought I cannot bear
And if God please my life to spare
I hope I shall reward thy care,   My Mother.

When thou art feeble, old, and grey,
My healthy arm shall be thy stay;
And I will soothe thy pains away,   My Mother.

And when I see thee hang thy head,
'Twill be my turn to watch thy bed ;
And tears of sweet affection shed,   My Mother.

For God who lives above the skies,
Would look with vengeance in his eyes
If I should ever dare despise,   My Mother.

PRAYERS.

A Morning Prayer.

GLORY to thee, O Lord! who hast preserved me from the perils of the night past, who hast refreshed me with sleep, and raised me up again to praise thy holy name.

Incline my heart to all that is good: that I may be modest and humble, true and just, temperate and diligent, respectful and obedient to my superiors; that I may fear and love thee above all things; that I may love my neighbour as myself, and do to every one as I would they should do unto me.

Bless me, I pray thee, in my learning: and help me daily to increase in knowledge, and wisdom, and all virtue.

I humbly beg thy blessing upon all our spiritual pastors and masters, all my relations and friends [*particularly my father and mother, my brothers and sisters, and every one in this house*]. Grant them whatsoever may be good for them in this life, and guide them to life everlasting.

I humbly commit myself to thee, O Lord! in the name of Jesus Christ my Saviour, and in the words which he himself hath taught me. *Our Father, &c.*

An Evening Prayer.

GLORY be to thee, O Lord! who hast preserved me the day past, who hast defended me from all the evils to which I am constantly exposed in this uncertain life, who hast continued my health, who hast bestowed upon me all things necessary for life and godliness.

I humbly beseech thee, O heavenly Father! to pardon whatsoever thou hast seen amiss in me this day, in my thoughts, words, or actions. Bless to me, I pray thee, whatsoever good instructions have been given me this day: help me carefully to remember them and duly to improve them: that I may be ever growing in knowledge, and wisdom, and goodness.

I humbly beg thy blessing also upon all our spiritual pastors, and masters, all my relations and friends [*particularly my father and mother, my brothers and sisters, and every one in this house*]. Let it please thee to guide us all in this life present, and to conduct us to thy heavenly kingdom.

I humbly commit my soul and body to thy care this night: begging thy gracious protection and blessing, through Jesus Christ our only Lord and Saviour, in whose words I conclude my prayer. *Our Father, &c.*

Grace before Meals.

SANCTIFY, O Lord! we beseech thee, these thy productions to our use, and us to thy service, through Jesus Christ our Lord. *Amen.*

Grace after Meals.

BLESSED and praised be thy holy name, O Lord, for this and all thy other blessings bestowed upon us, through Jesus Christ our Lord. *Amen.*

THE END.

Engraved and Printed by Edmund Evans, Racquet Court, Fleet Street, E.C.